YES TO G

YES to GOD

ALAN ECCLESTONE

ABBEY PRESS
St. Meinrad, Indiana 47577
1975

First published in Great Britain in 1975 by
Darton, Longman & Todd Limited
85 Gloucester Road, London SW7 4SU

© Alan Ecclestone

Library of Congress Catalog Card Number: 75-19923
ISBN: 0-87029-050-9
Printed in the U.S.A.
Abbey Press
St. Meinrad, Indiana

for Delia

'But you like none, none you, for constant heart.'

Contents

Introduction

'So then, he'd say: "Bridges! bridges! bridges! Use your bridges woman. It took thousands of years to build them, use them!"'
Arnold Wesker, *Roots*.

WHAT DO WE MEAN BY SAYING YES TO GOD? THERE IS, IT appears, an age-old ambiguity about this Yea or Yes, which no doubt reflects the difficulty of saying it at all. Modern man may hesitate over the word God. He is inclined to protest that it means too many things or that it is quite meaningless. His forbears felt more sure of God but much more diffident about admitting Yes. Some languages we learn had no such word, and we who use it often know quite well how dangerous and deceptive it can be. Oliver Wendell Holmes wrote in a pleasant fashion of his landlady's daughter whose 'Yes?' could put all things in question, and Byron more emphatically if cynically declared that women answering yes meant no and no meant yes. For many people yes appeared to mean too little or too much, to stand in need of qualification or supporting oaths. It was for Jesus Christ a matter of some importance too. He bid men answer plainly yes or no. He knew, we must believe, what doubts, heart-searchings and difficulties attended on the uttering of such words, and for this reason we begin by taking Him to be the first and fundamental answer to our question.

We mean by Yes to God, in the first place then, the life of Jesus Christ. That life, we understand as best we may, to have been a human life lived out at every point in true deliberate willing serviceable response to God. It meant attending on Him in his prayers; a constant searching out from day to day of what he should be doing, saying and thinking to read the purposes of God aright and do them. It meant envisaging his life as sent for a specific purpose. It meant decisions freely taken and abided by until the end. It was a Yes that kept its word with Death because both life and death were subject to the Father. It was in yet much more

I

mysterious fashion a Yes to men; a Yes pronounced by God Himself towards His creatures to make it clear how He regarded them, not merely creatures – though how dare we say 'merely' of the handiwork of God? – but creatures loved so much that He would take them through the Yes of Jesus Christ to be participants in His glory and heirs of His eternal life.

We mean, because of this, the Yes pronounced in human history by men and women who have endeavoured so to shape their lives as to conform as truly as they could to that pattern He had set. This is the Yes of the christian Church, the Body of Christ, learning and doing through the centuries what it believed to be the right response to God in the different social and cultural scenes in which it found itself. It took many and various forms; heroic in the brave witness of hopeful, faithful and loving men and women, imaginative in the proud architecture of its institutions, worship and theology, fearful in its distrust of criticism and new knowledge, arrogant in its self-confidence and possession of power. Like the voice of many waters its yes was turbulent, wasteful, energetic and magnificent. Near its source it spoke joyfully of its origin in Him. 'In Christ' men regarded themselves as made workers together in that labour that the Holy Spirit unceasingly performed to bring that Yes of Christ to the fullness of its consummation, the Yes that spanned the Alpha and Omega of the creation. 'The Son of God, the Christ Jesus that we proclaimed among you – I mean Silvanus and Timothy and I – was never Yes and No: with Him it was always Yes; and however many the promises God made, the Yes to them all is in Him.' Long after the sharp particularity of those promises or the astounding confidence that God had indeed made them had faded from men's minds, the zest for life that they had inspired continued to animate successive generations. As the Church itself broke into many pieces, its unity exchanged for chaos, its affirmations in sad dispute among the so-called members of one Body, the Yes of Christ remained, waiting upon men's needs, despair and sense of crisis, enduring in the bodies and minds of those who humbly endeavoured to approach Him.

The Yes to God means something more. There is the right response that all creation could be said to yearn to make, the creaturely desire, however buried and distorted it may be at times, to be itself, to be the work of God, which with a fine audacity the writer of Genesis will describe as being 'very good'. Right faith in God expects it to be so expressed. 'Sing, O ye heavens; for the Lord hath done it: shout, ye lower parts of the earth; break forth into singing, ye mountains, O forest, and every tree therein; for the Lord hath redeemed Jacob, and glorified himself in Israel.' This is the Yes that every man and woman, inside and outside churches, inside other faiths or none at all, will by striving to be human express in some degree in unremembered acts or in self-giving with a dedicated life. Its roots are in compassion, appreciation, delight and tenderness and love. Its growth is manifest in works of mercy, healing, education, justice, social welfare, respect for things and creatures of every kind. Its flowering is in art and science, in marriage, parental love and all commitment to delighted patient use of human powers.

There still remains a special aspect of the Yes to God, not separate from these three, the Christ, the Church, the Created world, but one which penetrates and embraces them all. This is the Yes of prayer, of prayer of every kind, for though we are here concerned in the main with christians trying to say Yes to God, that Yes today would be deplorably poor if it did not take account of other traditions of prayer and spirituality. Christian theology will remind us in its teaching about the Holy Spirit that such praying is ceaselessly at work, that our 'infirmity', inadequacy, ignorance and pitiful indisposition is less important than the fact that the great Wrestler Himself is so engaged. We should remind ourselves that all our theological formulations are no more than guides to the grappling with reality in living, and put to other uses usurp the freedom that properly belongs to those made in the image of God. As christians we recall the Yes to God Christ prayed and taught His friends to pray with Him. Without doubt we have hardly begun as yet to possess ourselves of and be possessed by the length and breadth of such a Yes. In prayer as in most other things we stand at all times in need of remembering Faber's warning that the measure of men's minds can be a grotesque narrowing of the love of God and of the response that men are invited to make to it. Without doubt the world itself breaks into prayer in exclamations and reflections of most varied kinds. The trees of the wood continue to rejoice and the stones cry out unheard by human ears. There are many people today who are concerned to widen and extend our consciousness of these and other manifestations of the Reality with which human life is invested. A greater measure of sifting and evaluating is needed to accompany the openness of mind that this bespeaks. It is the job of prayer to assimilate the stuff of all experience and to look beyond. The Yes to God of prayer not only gathers up all things that are, the light and dark, the pain and joy, the ventures and the failures, life and death, but launches out the one who prays into the deeps transcending these. In prayer we answer yes to what we've managed to face in life so far by learning to share in the Yes in Christ. It involves us no less in going on further to the yet unspoken unseen unimaginable Yes whither He is gone before.

This four-fold Yes is thus so vast that any book must be exposed by its short-comings. We can but try to look at certain things which in our own day do demand our noticing with special care, to be attentive in a special way to those revealing things in current experience that hitherto have not been so regarded. What follows here is governed by that purpose. It can never be an easy task to relate the Christ, the Church, the World and ourselves in prayer in such a way or ways that true enrichment follows. Far better to recognise at once that we are an under-developed people and see our true image in the so-called backward peoples of the world, in immigrants, the displaced, the squatters, the refugees, the 'Syrian ready to perish'. Then it is that we may hope to come to ourselves and to know not only our impoverishment but also something more of our inheritance, of the sonship to which we are called, of the resources we must learn to use. Von Hügel spoke often of self-starvation as the peril of the spiritual life, and much of his wise counselling was given to urging 'mutual help and mutual supplementation between the religious life and man's other powers, opportunities, needs, tasks and environments'. He loved to use the illustration of a confluence of rivers that has run through and drained a wide expanse of countryside as the proper image of rich spiritual life. He dreaded the concentrated narrowness of absorption in ecclesiastical affairs. No less deliberately we must use the figure of both building and using bridges of communication at a time when human life is threatened by the obliteration or paralysis of men's language-device and stored media of literacy. When men put to death the Incarnate Word they prefigured all those mockeries and contemptuous spittings, those thrusts of malice and silencing of lips, by which the spirit is set at nought, the cry is choked, and the bond between human beings is cancelled. About all our pretensions to utterance we have need to recall one line from *Loves Labours Lost*: 'This is not generous, not gentle, not

humble', a reminder that men all too easily grow arrogant, intoler-
ant and mean-spirited, not least when they presume to speak of
spiritual things.

It would be foolish to suppose that this essay is innocent of
such faults or that it can do much more than draw attention to its
own insufficiencies. It is but a plea for the utmost generosity of
mind that may enable us to make much fuller use in prayer of
what the artist and the poet, the student of society, the teacher and
the parent, the philosopher and the lover can give us to help in
our assimilation of the experience of human life today. We need
them all. The times are times of crisis, the enterprise is urgent.
We cannot afford to, we have no right to, leave unused in our
attempts to join in a faithful Yes to God now the help that all
these can give us. We need them specially to tell us what things
they have seen and heard. This book is but the gentlest plucking of
your sleeve, not to draw attention to itself, but to the greater
amplitude of prayer that we must strive to make our own.

I Words We Take With Us

'The Gracehoper was always jigging a jog, hoppy on akkant of his joyicity.'   James Joyce, *Finnegans Wake*.

'The Christian follows a master who bore a heavy burden; he has no ambition for the vain excercise of power and temporal eminence; he is the burden-bearer of creation.'
                                        Daniel Halévy, *Péguy*.

TO PRAY IS TO SEEK TO BE ENLIGHTENED. IT SPRINGS from the need to share with another those occasions of joy and sorrow and perplexity and fear that enter our lives. 'Look at this,' says the one who prays, 'that in the light of your regard for it I may see it the better.' Prayer holds a man and his concerns of whatever kind as much as it can in the light of God and His Truth. It confesses a trust that seen in that light 'all manner of things shall be well'. It is true, even so, that we neither desire to come to the light as much as we need nor know how to pray as we ought. Yet prayer remains the means by which we grope our way towards that which alone can satisfy that profoundest need of our human life to know we are known and loved by God.

Growing older, we do not find it any easier to pray. Our failing powers of body and mind, our knowledge of the turmoil in which we are involved, our remembrance of frequent failures in the past, all join together to weaken our attempts to go on doing it at all. No longer 'towering in the confidence of twenty-one', we find it harder to begin again, and praying, we have discovered, is always a matter of beginning again. 'With foot less prompt to meet the morning dew', we have to set out with just such deliberate purpose as once informed our more vigorous effort. The life of prayer is not a journey in which we note successive milestones passed, but one in which we set out once again from our departure point, going up with gladness to the holy city or going down sick at heart, as the case may be, with greater knowledge of the joy and pain involved.

Long-established habits do their best for us, but habits however good, can do no more than habits are devised to do, and praying wants to do more than this. Prayer seeks to break new ground. Prayer wants a world made new. Prayer tries to find its own authentic voice. The great books on prayer and meditation, the classics of the spiritual life, will help at times, and leave us glad and grateful for their wisdom. They too, however, can also leave us finding that we are not now the persons who can use or profit by their excellent advice. Their words are unexceptionably good; they might well have inspired us deeply had we not been so inert and dull and resistant to all inspiration. Our very familiarity with them as the years go by begins to mock our efforts to observe them once again. We are not the persons who once warmed to such direction. Not even the Lord's Prayer, it seems, at times can take possession of our random being and give it steadiness towards and hold on Him to whom we want to turn. We simply cannot do the thing we would. It is an old and commonplace experience, and no easier to bear for that. Charles Péguy thought that the 'Ave Maria' was our last resource. 'With that,' he said, 'you can't be lost.' But that too would be for very many still a form of words, of words that failed them in a desperate hour.

It is not to be supposed then that any book, and certainly not this one, could solve our problem and enable us to pray as our hearts long to do. Praying is too great a venture of the spirit in Man to be delivered from its difficulties like that. A book of such a kind has not been written nor ever can be, for praying comes not as a problem to be solved but as a venture to be lived out. It is so difficult a thing because it attempts so much. In prayer, Man sets his sights upon the Infinite. What could he expect but to discover over and over again that he is lost? He launches this pleasing anxious limited being upon a sea that knows no bounds in time or space. Small wonder that he finds himself beset by fears and darkness, by the dread feeling that he has lost his way, by suspicion that no way is to be found. Or he may, of course, protest that his intentions are more modest. All that he asks or seeks to do is but to speak in friendly trustful fashion with his Father in Heaven. 'No more but so?' But prayer itself is not a rockpool but an ocean. It is entirely right that men and women should venture themselves upon it with such trust. It is also right that they should learn, as learn they must, that those who pray must be inured by storms and tempered by great strains. 'Bid me come to Thee' is fine, but he

8

must needs pass through the waves who is taken at his word and bidden to do so. The waves are not less terrible in being subject to His word.

We begin then with a note of caution, reminding ourselves that words will work no magic, and that prayer itself is not to fix results but to enable us to come into the light, to see things as they are in that true light which is His Glory. Such words as we endeavour to use must be the most honest words that we can find, and Hamlet may remind us of the difficulties in attempting to do that. The words we choose can do no more than indicate a line to follow, a line that may bring us face to face with those features of our human life that praying must take hold of more deliberately, more confidently, more hopefully, than it has been doing in the past. A time of crisis such as ours demands a new deliberate effort to define or describe more clearly the nature of our most pressing tasks, to give men insight into what is most significant about the situation that they face. We pray that we may see. 'Take with you words, and turn to the Lord', Hosea's advice of long ago, is relevant still. The words we propose to take are two: engagement and passion.

Engagement presents us with a multitude of meanings right away, and one of these is that which turns upon a Yes of some considerable importance. A man and woman engage themselves to marry. An engagement day is a turning-point in life, and though we ordinarily think of the engagement or betrothal giving place to something else when the wedding-day comes round, it is plain that these two people have only just begun to be engaged with each other, and as a couple with life, as never before. Were it not a mechanical figure, and therefore one feebly incompetent to express the strange intricacies of human involvement, we might say that such a couple were now like gears engaged, now fitting sweetly in some common purpose, now grating hideously in misunderstanding. Engagements are of numerous other kinds. Each person who signs a contract, takes a vow, makes an appointment, crosses swords with another, fights battles or gets entangled and absorbed in play is thus engaged. We seek to telephone and find the line engaged; communication stops, there is no answer to our cry. In all these things there is a pledging or wagering of something or person, the mortgaging of life itself, the bet of faith. With just as many of these meanings as we can keep in mind, let's recognise that praying is engagement too, the most far-reaching in

9

intention, the most weighty in implication, the most rich in promise.

With passion we are on different but no less extensive ground. Both body and mind are equally involved, with storms and ecstasies as evidence to show for it. Wild, violent, tender, ugly, zealous gusts and currents of such passion can inspire and overwhelm our selves. We are 'carried away by passion', convulsed or blinded by it. But passion is also the suffering in our midst, the seed-bed of our patience. To bear it we become both passive and resistant, opposing quiet endurance to the storms of vehement grief or anger or desire. With passion we can be swept away, with no less passion we can hold our ground. Inset within the history of the world, the record of men's passions at work, is the Passion of Jesus Christ. The christian faith confronts us with the narratives of that Passion whose features have formed the groundwork of meditation and prayer for all succeeding generations. The emblems of that Passion are wrought in stone and wood and glass and paint throughout the world. For men like Paul, the Passion of Jesus Christ was the mainspring of converted life, the cardinal event upon which the world's salvation turned. The dialectic of that Passion, the death and life pronounced together, informs and shapes all christian prayer and living. Nor is awareness of it limited to those who are called christians. Imaginative work of such a kind as Bulgakov's novel *The Master and Margarita* can see the life of modern man silhouetted against the Passion of Christ. Prayer too is a matter of passion, of His and ours. His Passion was not simply accompanied by prayer, it was His prayer. Our praying likewise seeks to present these passionate wayward selves of ours to God through Him whose Passion claims to embrace them all.

Our two words must be kept together if they are to point to any reality in living. Engagement without passion is a heartless hoax, a mere formality that one day shows itself to have been no engagement at all, for there is no real engagement of ourselves with others that is not costly. The more deeply we are engaged, whether in marriage or the religious life, in parenthood or work of any kind, the more the active and passive elements of passion are tried out and put to use. Passion without engagement is a display of fireworks, a waste of energy, a self-abuse, 'full of sound and fury, signifying nothing'. It burns itself out to leave only ashes. Its intensity can scorch and scar but not transfigure. It knows and offers no guide to the worth of what it touches. Its most unlovely forms appear in sexual jealousy and religious bigotry, its most arid in sentimentality and wishful thinking. It can distort and wreck the best engagements of men's lives by vehement importunity and blind desire.

What matters then is what men are engaged in, what consumes their passionate intensity. The history of the world makes sombre reading on this theme. 'I have described,' wrote Gibbon, summing up his great *History of the Decline and Fall of the Roman Empire*, 'the triumph of Barbarism and Religion.' Wars, getting food and families, building cities, crafts and commerce, erecting monuments and writing books and worshipping their gods, have occupied mankind in slow and painful fashion. Destruction has trodden hard upon the heels of creativity. Arnold Toynbee out-Gibbons Gibbon by writing that 'the peace-making of the war-winners is the worst of all the calamities that War inflicts on those who perpetrate it'. Most human beings hitherto born have known but little more than a struggle to remain alive. In some more favoured times and places a glimpse of beauty, a shout of joy, an exclamation of wonder, a tenderness of feeling, a thought of wisdom, has broken through the carapace of custom, braved destruction, nurtured hope and humanised mankind a little. Engagement for life's sake has been at best an intermittent thing.

Today such human effort is world-wide in scope, more closely organised, more powerfully equipped and directed by more conscious purpose than at any time before. Concerted acts of thought and enterprise on scales undreamt of and of complexity inconceivable in an earlier age now open up the prospects of accelerative change throughout the world. Men's engagements with each other, with themselves and with the earth they live on, are such as to excite legitimate marvelling at the Ascent of Man and to raise anxiety about Man's moral fitness to meet the problems of his own fulfilment so added to and made more pressing by his vast achievements. It has not escaped his notice that at no time in his previous history has this engagement with nature, fellowmen and selfhood been more charged with problems, more compulsive, more suggestive of possibilities of good and evil. A weary irony proclaimed its cultural sophistication a Waste Land, an outraged youth denounced it as a lousy world, the teeth of boredom gnawed at all its institutional props, the spectre of 'the man who no longer responds to any spiritual appeal, who lacks even the ability to do so' arrived to haunt the heirs of the Century of Hope.

Meanwhile a passionate intensity was evoked to spit on freedom, to ravage the good earth, to plan and execute with bestial ingenuity the mass-extermination of rejected peoples. A reckless brinkmanship played hard for superiority in possession of weapons of mega-destructive scale.

In the darkened hours of His Passion the Son of Man, having known the bitterness of disengagement to the full, having borne the burden of creation to its end, yielded up His spirit in a final Yes to God. Prayer makes its way at such a time as this within the Yes of Christ, the Yes that will not let mankind be wrenched apart from God. It thus insists on looking not away from but more closely at the world in which His Passion is wrought out. It seeks, as Mother Julian sought, to see the details of such passionate engagement in the actual everyday experience of men and women. Prayer strives to penetrate through what to eyes of un-engagement must be baffling and repellent, too hard to understand, too cruel to endure, too meaningless to use, in order to discern the lines of the emergent work, the future of Man being shaped, and in order to engage the one who prays with what is being wrought. Such indeed is the spiritual intention of Teilhard de Chardin, presenting in *The Phenomenon of Man* a vision of 'an ever more highly organised consciousness' operating in mankind to attain its full consummation in the Omega point of Christ, and calling upon men to strive to see and exult in seeing how they themselves were summoned to be doing a great work from which, like Nehemiah, they were not to be called away. It is the job of praying to refuse to be disengaged.

Prayer seeks the elucidation of what being so engaged with The Yes of God to man both asks of us and gives. The prior condition of rich generous praying is an openness of heart and mind, an absence of defensive rigidity in dealing with experience, an avoidance of preconceived distinction between the spiritual life and life subject to and stamped by all the pressures of the world. Such prayer at no time is detached from living in the world, for how we pray depends to no small extent upon the way we are already acting in it. A spirituality that is not so open is being starved of its necessary food, and becomes misshapen, precious, subject to all kinds of fantasy, and unwilling to adventure its gifts in acts of faith. The prayer of openness to full engagement with God's world is so demanding, so completely testing of the willingness of every man and woman to commit themselves in faith, so utterly a venture into the unknown, that it is not surprising that spiritualities have, as often as not, contrived to become inturned, legalistic, miserly and unexpectant. All too often a narrowly ecclesiastical or clerical version of the good life and prayer has in the past drawn to itself the energy and devotion that should have entered freely into the common life of men. Hoarding the seed of the spirit indicates a disastrous lack of faith in its ability to fall into the ground and die and rise to new life. However good the spiritual crop already stored up may be – our liturgies, offices, psalms, hymns and spiritual songs, treasuries of devotion and methods of prayer – what matters more than these is the sowing for the harvest still to come. It means exposing the life of the spirit to harsh raw lacerating conditions, learning to live off the land as the journey goes on, losing and being willing to lose things of great value, 'having nothing but possessing all things'. Worldliness in the evil sense of that word has already corrupted the souls that are afraid of venturing into the world or to let go what they now prize. The prayer that responds to the Yes of Christ goes into that world expecting to meet Him. Paul Klee once spoke of his work as an artist in words that will fit all ventures of faith. 'One leaves the realms of here and now and builds forwards into the beyond where there is still a possibility of a relative Yes.'

Our prayer begins then with acknowledgement of God's engagement of Himself with this world of men. As Newman said of Christianity, 'its home is in the world; and to know what it is, we must seek it in the world, and hear the world's witness of it'. The hardest part of that witness lies in its rejection of it, in the No which is shouted by the world in reply to God, in the chorus of pitiful Nos that we all are invited to join in. It is here that the Passion again and again must be felt in our praying, the marks of it seen in the things we observe. We are all still capable of looking on at some new revelation of His Passion in our midst, and crying out that if only He would extricate Himself from such disgusting circumstances we would believe in Him. Our Yes would be forthcoming promptly if His were not so mingled with the mire and blood, but such a yes that we might make would be too thin and shallow for the claims He makes on us. He so engaged Himself in earth and flesh and blood, in men's sickness and despair, in their rejoicing and their terror, that they might be engaged in turn with His eternal life, that is, with life not measured out in years or in possessions or in power but life so confident in loving that they were ceaselessly renewed by it. He took our flesh that in and through this flesh the infinite riches of His glory might be known. He lodged His Yes in human history, in human culture, in man's make-up, institutions, words and deeds. The Yes He looks for must as surely make its way through all these things with patient purpose to refine and purify them all. It is with men's discouragements that spirituality must be geared to deal. 'How hard it is,' cried Kierkegaard, reflecting on this task, 'in praying to reach the Amen. For though to the man who has never prayed it looks easy enough to get quickly through with it yet to the man who had a longing to pray and began to pray the experience must have occurred that he constantly felt as if there were something more upon his heart, as if he could not get everything said, or get it said as he would like to say it, and so he does not reach the Amen.' There is in fact no final Amen we can make. The Yes begins as often as we address ourselves to it again. The beginning was not in ourselves but in Him. So too the end. The best that we can hope to do is tentative and provisional always – 'Earth's young significance is all to learn' – a process of finding out in the context of ordinary secular events and through our participation in them those pointers to the divine truth which men in other ages discerned in their contemporary conditions. In Norwegian storytelling there is a phrase descriptive of continuing journeying through great distances, 'from one blue to another'. So is it with our prayer. The further 'blue' is not a mockery of our efforts but promise of infinity. What matters most in praying is not the yes that could round off neatly what was there begun, but that continuing conversation that bears within itself the Gracehoper's joyicity in discovering that Yes means more and more.

We have then to consider deeply how at such a time as this the praying that we try to do is to be shaped. What things, for instance, shall we take to be the evidence of things not seen, the substance of the Glorious Mystery that faith discerns? We have but to reflect on what makes up the greater part of the devotional action of our churches to realise how little it is open to renewal, how much is occupied with imagery and metaphor gone dead, how little people engaged in it are really being themselves at every point. A dread of 'things getting out of hand', an absence of hopeful expectancy, a lack of theological inquiry, is so common in the average parish congregation in Britain that neither a restless younger generation wanting to use its own idioms of expression but with no very clear idea of what it wants to use them for, nor an older body of people conscious that they must somehow learn to pray better though they fear to let go what they have for so long been used to, is being helped. It is not the case that stirrings of the Spirit are lacking. Charismatic renewal with its various manifestations overleaping denominational fences, experiments in group living, militancy on behalf of causes and oppressed people, demonstrations expressive of both anger and delight, festivities of an imaginative kind, surge and swirl throughout society today. The greatest danger lies not in the 'emotionalism' that pervades the situation but in the likelihood that so much of the emotion will be dissipated long before it can be put to use in changed styles of living, or will be channelled off into freak groups that have little contact with the main body of the Church. *Jesus Christ Superstar* is but one example of imaginative use of the media available to and resonant of this turbulent situation, making the religious films and shows that the Church had generally been associated with look like *Gorboduc* or *Ralph Roister Doister* compared with *Hamlet* or *Hedda Gabler*. Again, it is not the case that men and women of great artistic gifts are not there to be used. The trouble lies deeper. Neither new nor older forms of art can go on simply illustrating the already accepted statements of religious faith, the Yes to God of past generations. They must transform, transfigure and press more deeply into whatever they touch. They must be searching for the Yes that is to be made today and tomorrow. If that Yes appears to be a very considerable No to much that has been accepted hitherto, it will no doubt be hard to take it. But if the engagement and the passion are of the character that the christian faith declares them to be, there is something wrong in their presentation if they are not hard to take, not once but over and over again in our lives. It is because so many people think that they know what the Nativity and Passion of Jesus Christ are saying to the world and have grown so used to conventional forms that excite no difficulties for them, that their spirituality remains inert. They do not expect to be reduced to silent agonising searching prayer at the end of a play on the Birth or Death of the Christ. They can neither laugh with joy nor cry with pain. They cannot go into travail with the Yes to God that must be reborn in them. The piercing sword that compels the utterance of the thoughts of many hearts does not disturb them. The great hope that this is indeed the truth of our life does not sweep in like a tide once again to refresh and renew. Bad money drives out the good. The defaced currency of conventional religious imagery excites no amazement at the Yes of God.

Yet the primary business of prayer is to be attentive to and dwell upon that Yes of God that gives, sustains, redeems and loves the whole creation. It grows by what it perceives. It withers when we cease to be responsive to or aware of God at work; it is enfeebled if divorced from continuous wrestling with those things which challenge the profession of faith. What too often is missing from the life of the local church, the matrix of our spiritual lives, and no doubt from that of religious communities, is the concerted operation of all its members to scrutinise, sift and take common possession of all that is available in current experience for the nurturing of God's people. There can be little use in quoting the description of the Church as a body if each several part does not share in the nourishment, equipment, discipline and work of the whole body. This applies with special force to prayer which needs to be seen with new intensity today as shared prayer or what the old name of common prayer suggested but did not always arrive at, the prayer that binds together successive generations, diverse, friendly, hostile people not simply at a particular point in time but as part of the ongoing action of the Incarnation itself. Such shared prayer cannot rely upon a common form to do what is needed. It may use as far as it can traditional resources, but it must be also free to transform them to meet new needs. It must help to unlock and free the movements of the spirit among those who are drawn together and not be afraid of the difficulties it runs into. This burden-bearing of creation cannot go on without the prayer that keeps pace with the movements and haltings, struggles and bafflements, that belong to what Vladimir Lossky rightly describes in terms of conquest. In a time like ours when the generation-gap seems wider than ever before, it is good to note in the preparation that we make for prayer the words of the ending of the book of Malachi taken up in the angel's message in the opening of the Gospel of St Luke, for this turning of the hearts of the fathers to the children and the hearts of the children to their fathers is no smoothing down of the hostilities and tensions which spring into life between the generations, but the costly seeking out of an understanding that bears all the marks of the Passion. This is but one example of what von Hügel described as a necessity for powerful religious life of 'friction, tension, rivalry, mutual help and mutual supplementation between this religious life and man's other powers, opportunities, needs, tasks, environments', and therefore between the men and women who express these things in their lives and prayers. There are tensions and frictions enough in churches but how rarely of this kind?

How then do we get hold of this? To turn the hearts of the fathers to the children is not only to face the generation-gap but to take one's own heart back to the beginning of its journey, not in Peter Pan-ish fashion refusing to grow up but seeking to be reborn with new energy, with new sense of relationship, with new receptiveness to the working of the Spirit of God. 'Only after the Last Judgment,' wrote Péguy, 'will beginning again come to an end.' In the meanwhile the foundation of our personal effort to pray must be that communion of all those men and women in and through whom the Spirit works. Our new beginnings lie in the whole length and breadth of this cosmic operation which in the world today is being seen with new eyes, and which needs to be recognised with new joy by those who make up the holy community of each christian congregation. For we who now live at this present time have particular reason for such celebration. We have especial cause to rejoice. We can look back and see how, as the modern world developed, the christian Churches failed to grasp the problems raised by so many aspects of its life, and grew less and less able to inform the kind of prayer men needed to make in such a world. Whole areas of human life in industry, technology and scientific thought slipped out of reach of the traditional forms of prayer. Neither with penitence nor with joy could men grasp the spiritual implications of the world they were so swiftly building. The learning process by which they might be prepared to say Yes to God in their new-made world was slow and fitful and often checked. Sectarian pride and jealousy and fear hemmed in and choked the responsiveness so sorely needed. Much of that fearful legacy remains with us today but nevertheless a new beginning has been made. As the Vatican Declaration on religious freedom has indicated it is recognised that the Church must with a new humility be ready to learn from both non-religious movements and religious traditions other than its own. 'The consciousness of contemporary man' must be among the sources of its enlightenment that it may learn to know more fully both what mankind so desperately needs and what resources God has given for meeting them. As we learn to see ourselves as immigrants into a new world, we catch from one another perceptions of the truth that other faiths and spiritualities can bring. There are 'so many kinds of voices in the world, and none of them is without signification'. In Thomas Merton's journey to the East there was a sense of urgency entirely in keeping with the gravity and the grace-hoping condition of humankind today. We cannot afford to neglect the insights and long experience of religious faith much older than our own, nor can we pray with purity of heart until there is purged from us that evil spirit that prompted persecution. No more appalling image of Christ's Passion in the world has been presented to us than that continued age-long persecution of the Jews in christian Europe. Failing to honour the distinctiveness of Jewry, the christian Church has weakened its own power of learning what it means to be the people of God in a hostile or indifferent world. It has failed again and again to live out the implications of an Exodus theology, and to be warned by the facts of the Exile.

In welcoming the changes that have marked the decade now behind us we do not blur nor overlook the distinctiveness of our own calling in Jesus Christ, but rather recognise how His own will to draw men to Himself takes on new seriousness today and calls for changed response from those who bear His name. New every morning must be the attempted Yes. 'To live is to change,' wrote Newman, 'and to be perfect is to have changed much.' As we have learned to acknowledge in human life the recapitulation of those adaptive changes by which mankind has reached this present state, as we have now begun to train and retrain men and women for different jobs successively in life, so must we learn to fashion anew the Yes to God that springs from changed conditions. 'We seek a new world through old workings', and ever and again find ourselves arrested, checked, frightened and perplexed by the conditions we are compelled to face. Just over a century ago Newman wrote the famous *Grammar of Assent*. He was anything but a yes-man in the pejorative sense that the word now carries, but he knew far better than most christians of his time how great an effort was needed to shape an adequate Yes from modern man. The Yes he sought was much more sensitively moulded but no less robust than Carlyle's Everlasting Yea. It was braver and more generous in scope than most christian thinking of the time had dared to be. Newman was well aware that doubts were abroad, that beliefs once thought unassailable were being shaken, that men too lazy to think about their faith were in danger of losing it, and that Englishmen were perhaps rather specially inclined to be ill-disciplined if not something worse in matters of this kind. The spiritual heirs of Robinson Crusoe were ever ready to believe that they could manage to be 'an ilonde' unto themselves. Walter Bagehot put it more succinctly by remarking that 'in real sound stupidity the English are unrivalled'.

Newman guessed how ill-prepared men were to meet the impact of the changing world conditions on their faith and devotional life. He did not scrutinise those changes nor list suggestions as to how to meet them. He would most probably have welcomed all the light that sciences could throw upon the human scene, but his own work was of a different kind. The Yes he sought to nourish must come from men to whom the Yes of God had given a freedom they must learn to use. His work was perfectly attuned to this. His style was pure, his reasoning sound, his language musical and clear, but the engagement he sought to bring about and the passion that inspired him belonged not to the argument he pursued, but to the silence in which the Yes to God must be articulated. Newman approaches his readers with studied care, speaks with the greatest precision, and then with the gentlest gesture he is gone, withdrawn, effaced. All his great assemblage of propositions, professions, presumptions, real and notional assents, categorical, conditional and interrogative forms, fade out as unsubstantial things and we are left alone with God. 'At times we seem to catch a glimpse of a form which we shall hereafter see face to face.' As Brémond has reminded us, the essential Newman is expressed in 'Heart speaketh unto heart'. He is a guide to praying not so much for what he has to say about prayer but because when he has finished speaking about any matter, we are not his captives but men who know a little better what a Yes to God must mean.

Prayer is most truly prayer when it is uttered in the simplest way. There are some moments in the life of men and women, just as there are some rare persons who have such gift, when simplicity possesses heart and mind and mouth. For the rest, simplicity is something to be struggled for, to be worked away at, so that as our praying endeavours to assimilate the bewildering multiplicity of experience of the world, it strives to be as honest, discriminative, brave and sensitive as it can be. Best done in secret and in silence, it nevertheless draws all it can from openness to others and their needs and hopes and burdens. It needs to be as wide as life itself. The Yes in process of being uttered must be such as helps both men and women in their several lives as well as in their world-society to see the spiritual implications of what is going on around them, equip them to withstand corruption, enlarge their diligence for good, and make them hopeful and expectant of the future. It must set them free from the 'false consciousness' that cultural myths, political oppression, social prejudice and ideological presuppositions engender. Paulo Freire has given the name 'conscientization' to the overcoming of such falsification of men's grasp of the reality of life, and described it as a programme for cultural action for Latin America, and by implication for the whole Third World. The praying that we speak of now must lose no scrap of what he so describes but rather carry it further towards the conscientisation of all men everywhere. It must be freeing the spoiled children of the affluent society no less than the deprived. It must embrace the mighty and the poor as did Christ's mother in her Magnificat. Keeping pace as best it can with changes in man's life, it will endeavour to read the signs of the times and see and hear the Yes of God's engagement being newly uttered to His people in their changed conditions and ways of life.

Behind the effort to which prayer calls each of us today, within the crisis which demands of us a more far-reaching Yes than men have yet attempted, there lies the Amen we must learn to make our own. The Hebrew people used it with a passionate intensity at times, not only with their lips but in their lives, in all their journeying and captivity, their keeping of the Law and in their witness to God's presence. Through the years their Yes to God took on still deeper meaning as new generations faced the need to keep alive the hope of Israel's redemption. They sounded out in the extremities of their passion the possibilities of being able to continue to say Yes to God throughout. In a recent study of the work and teaching of Reb Menahem Mendl of Kotzk, known as the Kotzker, Abraham Heschel makes clear that the great Hasidic masters of the spiritual life did not wrestle in prayer in order to come up with an answer to the anguished confrontation with evil in the world but to possess themselves of the truth 'that in all their affliction He was afflicted'. Engagement and Passion come together in the compassion that binds God and man together. It is the business of such prayer to counter despair with hope. The Hebrew Amen must be translated as the expression of that hope – 'would that it might be so'. As such it is no tail-piece to a prayer but in itself the essence of the bond that binds together God and man. For christians it took on a greater meaning in the use made of it by Jesus Christ. The word, it is recorded, was often on his lips; the note of personal authority it marked was quite unique. There is no parallel, some scholars say, to usage of this kind elsewhere. 'Amen, I say to you', has been compared to the Old Testament phrase 'Thus saith the Lord', but with an added force of truth conveyed not simply in the message but in the Person of the one who used it. In Him the purpose of the Living God and the true response to it are one 'In the Amen before the "I say to you" of Jesus, the whole of Christology is contained'. It was the task of generations of His friends to spell out for themselves and for their world what their own Amen to Him would mean.

Such is our task today. As christians we need more than anything else experience comparable to that of the Hasidic movement in Jewry, in which the preparation for prayer took on a quite new depth. Prayer promises nothing but the staying with God. For far too long the christian world has lived at ease with its faith, assumed too lightly that it knew how to pray, and dealt too carelessly with the stuff out of which prayer is to be made. There are dark days ahead. The Kotzker taught that the preparation for prayer surpassed in spiritual value prayer itself. At all events we must begin again.

2 Prayer and Pain

'I think there's a pain somewhere in the room,' said Mrs
Gradgrind, 'but I couldn't positively say that I had got it.'
Charles Dickens, *Hard Times*.

'But from the tree of human pain
Redeem our sterile misery.'
David Gascoyne, *Poems 1937–42*.

VERY MANY REASONS ARE GIVEN FOR THE PRACTICE OF
prayer. We start here with the simple fact that a great many people
pray. They may do it badly, rarely, for very mixed reasons and
often in childish forms. They may never stop to ask themselves
why they do it at all, though they often ask questions about how
they could do it better. They may even be a bit apologetic about it,
a little ashamed to admit if questioned that they don't do as much
as once they did, or as they feel they ought to. They are more
numerous too than those who go to church. Today their numbers
include small groups of people who attach importance to learning
some ways of prayer and meditation by no means confined to the
christian tradition. The presence of Muslims, Sikhs, Buddhists and
members of other religious groups in our midst can kindle attention to such things. The decline or weakening of the older beliefs and practice of large numbers of christians in the West has
given more scope or reason for looking at other faiths and their
methods of prayer. Sociologists have made clear that unchurched
people avail themselves of the help of a number of substitute
faiths and creeds, and are catered for by teachers and prophets,
salesmen and gurus, of every imaginable kind. Somewhere within
all this, and even outside it, praying goes on. There is much to be
learned from its practice. Why do men pray?

To say that people have always prayed is not the most helpful
answer but it widens the scope of our inquiry. It saves us also
from assuming too easily that the phase of history that we know
as ours may be taken to represent all others or be the wisest and

22

most enlightened in such things that the world has ever known. Historical perspective, even if derived from one or other of the boring operations described by J. H. Hexter as 'tunnel history', enables us to see some things more clearly than we might otherwise do. It suggests that our opinions may be qualified and revised by knowledge if we are willing and humble enough to seek it. There, certainly, embedded in the practice of great nations and cultures of the past is prayer. Our earliest literatures are rich with forms of prayer; our tragedy derives from public festivals at which men stood before the altars of the Gods and prayed. Our European culture has roots deep in the Hebrew practices of prayer taken over and reshaped by christians of many nations for their common purpose. Our commonest links with bygone days are often words and phrases that have come to us through centuries of use in prayer. Our question now becomes, Why have men prayed?

It would be foolish to suppose that we could with any confidence reply. Confronted by the cave-pictures of Lascaux or Altamira, the expert is today more ready to say that he doesn't know what was in the minds of those who painted them. He is less ready than students of other days to advance a golden bough by which to interpret to us the meaning of ritual ceremonies and rites and dances. When it comes to words we may feel we are better equipped to follow for they may have had continuous use from ancient times till now. Translation, we think, has made them ours. Here too, however, the experts in semasiology will certainly warn us against any such reckless thought. We may pray, no doubt, with gestures and words like those men used three thousand years ago in conditions remote from our own, but dare we say, therefore, that we know what praying then meant to them? We may hazard an opinion as to why a vast crowd assembled to shout 'Great is Diana of the Ephesians', as we are told in the Acts of the Apostles they did, but can we guess at the complex strands of meaning that lay behind the shouts?

Prayers from the ancient world have survived in writing. We can read the words of supplication addressed to the Lord Serapis, to Isis and to Mithras, and discover how like they are to those we christians commonly use, but what did their users in a city of Asia Minor or a fort on Hadrian's Wall in Britain understand by them? There are a number of common desires and hopes shared by men and women throughout the ages. We believe we know a little of what David's lament for Absalom or the anguish of Jeremiah implies, for we catch the sound of a human voice expressive of human pain. But prayer is more than a list of requests or salutes or titles. We want to know what lies behind them. Across the usages of the past there creeps the chilling breath of decay. A generation arrives that finds them lifeless, and turns to some new teacher or faith for help. It cries 'Lord, teach us to pray'. Jeremias tells us that about the time of the beginning of the christian era there was a crisis of prayer in the Hellenistic world. Did confidence wane and why? Will it be always so? To answer our question at all we have to penetrate into the inmost shrine, to the place where prayer has once been valid, and discover for ourselves that this really means not buildings and holy places which remain as inscrutable as Karnak or Stonehenge, but the minds of the men who prayed. And there we may pause to consider how any such intimate thing as prayer can be thought to disclose to any inquirer what it really implied. How much do we know of our own selves in prayer? Before we can answer at all we must reflect on the people who prayed.

We may begin with the Hebrew foundation upon so much of which the christian Church has drawn, as men do when they use the hewn sculptured stones of an earlier age to build with for themselves. In this case, it is clear that whole sections have been removed *en bloc*, and though some obvious incongruities are there, a great deal of trouble has been taken to dovetail the old and new. The names, the request, the hopes sound very familiar. We ourselves, the advocates say, are the heirs of the promises made to this people and their story is part of our own. Their praying is the great matrix from which our devotion has drawn its life. We must needs examine it whenever we reconsider the praying we try to do.

In brief, it takes the form of a detailed recital of the things God did to call this people His own, to insist on a manner of living, to free them from oppression, to bless their life and punish their sins. Something distinctive in that deliberate care of God for this people, in the relations between Himself and them, passes over into their prayers and gives them a dynamic character. They are the community prayers of the people of God. Successive generations penetrate more deeply into the significance of that allegiance on their part, and of the infinite mercy of His. To pray is to acknowledge the fact of belonging to this people, to accept its standards of behaviour set out in its code, to rejoice in its successes, to bewail its shortcomings, to reiterate its hope. Such praying is always a great chorus that celebrates the epic of deliverance, that recalls in memory the great servants of God who played their part in it, that acclaims the triumphant events that marked its path. The man who prays does so as participating in a corporate confession of faith. His existence and survival, his well-being and happiness, depend so utterly upon belonging to this fellowship that he can do no more important thing than to bring it to mind in prayer. He answers our question by showing his dependence upon God who thus dealt with His chosen people.

But praying in Hebrew experience did not stop there, though at no time did it lose this primary character. It proceeded rather to distil from the experience it had known the fine essence of its relationship with God, and to derive from it a profound conception of the nature of God and man. Much may seem obvious in this until we compare it with the way in which we ourselves are accustomed to look at our own history, with the emphasis we put upon the aspect of objectivity, and with the likelihood that the lessons if any that we are disposed to draw from such history will be confined to politics and economics. To the Hebrew mind it was more important to look further, and the outcome of that meta-historical reflection was a spirituality so far-reaching, so patient of continuing meditation, that generations of men 'who knew not Joseph' or his people have found no better or more adequate guide to life. Both Jews and christians have extended it, relating it to their new conditions of life as best they could, but they have not put it aside. The use of the Psalms is an example of this. Men have drawn out with their help in what we call personal terms the implications of this people's relation to God, in faith and faithlessness, in freedom and captivity, in expectation and fulfilment. They have extended and transformed a people's creed into a conversation between man and God, a people's history into a revelation of the nature of God and man, a people's calling into an assertion of faith in man's destiny under God.

It is this intimate relationship which we call engagement that distinguishes this Hebrew praying. The initiative in it lay with God. The outstanding representative figures in their spiritual history understood themselves to be addressed and called upon to reply. Their praying is a response. Uttered with awe and consternation, wrung out at times from unwilling lips, it takes place again and again upon the very margins of human experience. It is never an exchange of formalities or counters in a conversational game. To do it at all a man took terrible risks. It committed him to matters of life and death. He might grovel, run away, hide himself or beg to be released. What it made clear was will and purpose, presence and memory, concern and love, all such intimate things that a man found not in himself but nevertheless learned to regard as the truth of his own being, summoned and quickened by this eliciting prayer. A man is what he prays.

This is the point at which the praying of Jesus must be looked at. It is with Him and 'the things concerning Jesus' in mind that the question Why pray? may be repeated. It is said that those who followed Him and observed His work and manner of life most closely asked Him to teach them His way of prayer, His distinctive way of doing it. To men of a praying people whose national life was stamped with the impress of fixed hours of prayer, moulded by an educational system which provided for disciplined approach to praying, and marked by the singular acts of such figures as Honi the Circle-Drawer believed to have power to bring rain, it was clear that He did something new. Whether so many of the things that He did and said were so novel and unique as some scholars would maintain is a question only scholars can pursue, and on that discussion rages. The Gospels themselves suggest that friend and foe alike were caught by His way of praying. For some it was an offence, for others disturbing enough to make them ponder, for a few it was a revelation of a new age breaking in.

Put in the terms of today we should say that it was both personal and universal in its bearing. Prayer could not have been made more personal than this. 'The God of Abraham, the God of Isaac and the God of Jacob, God great mighty and fearful, most high God, master of heaven and earth,' as the benediction of traditional prayer addressed Him, was in the terms of vernacular endearment called My Father, Our Father or just Father. Why pray? Because a father and son do want to talk to each other, because a father is greatly concerned for his son, because it matters what lies between them. The full force of this does not come home to us till the conversation between God and man is carried on in the intimate terms such as parents and lovers use. The public-address style, formal, dignified and a bit remote, has slipped away, and in its place we have, not simply the talking of friend to friend but something much more, the language of oneness in love. 'I know that Thou hearest me always.' It was and is the quite stagger-ing assertion of the christian faith that this is the truth of our life.

To call God Father, as Jesus taught men to do, is, even so, to use the language of poetry, and this men often forget. We live in a world that largely believes, as Dickens described Mr Gradgrind as doing, that the only language worth knowing is the language of facts. It pays a suspicious lip-service to poetical things. Like Audrey, in *As You Like It*, it's not quite sure that poetical is honest. Even the Church has joined in this way of suspecting the language of poetry. It has done so often because it has been afraid, as men were frightened by the behaviour of Jesus. It could not get rid of the language of poetry already there in its hymns and prayers and creeds, but it ceased to welcome and make much of what poetry does, which is to extend the language of oneness-in-love by finding new ways to use and enjoy it. It ceased to teach men to approach God in these terms. Poetry doesn't make ob-solete such images as those of fatherhood and families and wed-dings but it constantly gives them a new look. It is always daring men to see their life and world with newly opened eyes, to find new words to speak of them, as Jesus did. The imagery He used would itself moulder away unless its meanings were being re-newed and extended by a new poetical grasp of what it implies. So it is with all that mankind essays to know in physics, biology, psychology and kindred sciences. There is no other way to speak of what men seek but in pictures, metaphors and symbols, and these like all things that matter to living men must be reborn. What men perceive in Christ, how men pray through Christ, must likewise be re-spoken. We pray because there is no other way by which the unborn images can begin to take our flesh.

There is also the universal aspect of His prayer. The image He used to speak of it was that of the Kingdom of God, an expression we still use in our prayers though it may be doubted whether it now figures largely in exciting or compelling men to pray. Quite early in the history of the christian Church attention was shifted from the teaching of the coming of the Kingdom to the person of Christ and the significance of His death and resurrection. Though the Kingdom could have been said to come with Christ's work among men, the shift from the earth, the scene of His life among men, to the Godhead itself made for changes in praying which remain with us yet. The expectation of the appearance of the Kingdom upon earth, though supported by many of the early

Fathers was displaced by a purely mystical conception of the nature of the Kingdom and later by a tendency to identify the Kingdom with the Church. The change of outlook was deeply significant. Something in the imagery Jesus used to describe the coming of the Kingdom lost its sharp intensity for the majority of the members of the Church. The thief in the night, the reckoning with the servants, the marriage feast, the warning about the deluge, and such language now referred to as apocalyptic, became the characteristic expression of the hopes of the sects and sectarian pressure within and often against the official teaching of the Church. But it did not die. In spite of increasing condemnation and persecution of such millenarian movements, men turned in times of disaster and terror to the imagery of fearful conflict with the Anti-Christ upon earth, the overturning of all existing social order, and the coming of a new age in which the poor and oppressed inherited another Eden. The pursuit of the Millennium, as Norman Cohn and others have made clear, remained a disturbing factor in a life already precariously maintained, exploding in pogroms and crusades, renunciation of goods, wild camp meetings and violent ascetic practices, throughout the Middle Ages and down to our own times. In thinking of why and how men have prayed, this current of human expectation, however productive of and inspired by fantasy, cannot be ignored. Ever and again it breaks in upon the ordered scene of comfortable conventional practice as a sharp reminder of the suffering and pain not otherwise to be endured. In it the Passion cries aloud in its lowliest and most humiliated tones. In Latin America, Africa and Asia today, it may well be this aspect of prayer that commands the attention and energies of the great mass of humanity. Theirs is the response of those who cling to the tree of human misery in the hope that the poor shall not always be forgotten. It was such a tree that Jesus Christ Himself carried and made the substance of His prayer, His Yes to God. For those of us living in comfort it raises great questions we cannot ignore. If the praying of Jesus took its character from His conviction and announcement of the breaking in upon the world of God's new age, so that His prayer for daily bread and for the forgiveness of sins is prayer for the bread of the new life begun and the wholly new relationships set up, it may be questioned whether many of us pray after this manner at all. We have gone so far to accustom ourselves to living as though the Kingdom of our God and His Christ has become the political and social order that we approve of, and have grown so used to an idealised version of the christian life, that the imagery Jesus used tends to be treated as picturesque description, as so many set-pieces of a bygone world-view. This is a dangerous condition from which any Yes to God might be made. Imagery and words disengaged from the realities of living become, as we said earlier, openings for sentimentality, and it must always be a real part of the preparation for prayer to recognise how easily beset by temptations to indulge in sentimental reflection our praying can be. It was once said of Coleridge that he wanted better bread than could be baked from wheat. It is not difficult to persuade ourselves that we are hungering for the bread that cometh down from Heaven when we are merely dissatisfied with the bread we have been given already.

Between Christ's day and ours then, lies the long experience of the christian Church in the course of which the reasons for praying and the ways of prayer changed greatly. We can observe in the rich orthodox devotion of catholic christendom a superbly confident sense of an ordered universe, an economy of salvation, an etiquette of required behaviour, a careful provision of the means of grace. The Yes of each person within it is an instructed Yes. There is a firm objectivity about the ordering of the life of the household of the faith which at its best shaped selfless heroism of saintly life and at its worst encouraged shameless manipulation of holy things. There was room within it for the mystic, the theologian, the ascetic, the *jongleur de Dieu*, the poet and the philosopher. It knew and made much of prayer. It shaped a great practice of contemplative life, seeking through disciplined methods the vision of God. But there grew up within it a division of the life of the cloister from the life of the world. Contemplation became the prerogative of the 'religious' life, of the monk and the nun. A higher and lower standard of devotion attached itself to prayer. To that distinction may be traced the fact that throughout the greater part of the Middle Ages men did not write books to help and encourage those 'living in the world' to pray. The model of praying was that of the clerk. That is not to say that popular devotion could not have been vigorous and rich, spilling over from the vast enterprise of monks and nuns into the lives of men and women, whether kings or merchants, soldiers or craftsmen, ploughmen or poets. Most clearly it was. It blazed into life in love and reverence for the Virgin-Mother. In that great ordered universe subjected to eternal law, she was the personally free source of immediate and tender love. Men sought her aid because they yearned for something other than equity and justice. They wanted protection, forgiveness, comfort, counsel as children do, and they turned their prayers to the Mother, to the Woman, to the Queen of Heaven, to declare their needs. Her engagement with their lives was clear. This second Eve was mother of them all. She knew and understood their needs. We answer our question as to why men prayed at this time by observing what the American historian Henry Adams described as the pathos of the Gothic cathedral, in which exuberant delight flung up towards the sky its vaults and spires while it buried its self-distrust and anguish of doubts deep in the earth. Such joy and pain sought in its prayer the knowledge and assurance of maternal love.

But this is not by any means the whole truth of men's need to pray. Men go to God, as a poem of Bonhoeffer sets out, for many reasons, and among them we find one that recurs throughout the ages of faith as a protest against a superficial huckstering with God. Not anguish, not doubt, not a simple delight or joy, but hunger for reality takes hold of men and women driven to ponder on the nature of their lives and impels them to use prayer to penetrate below and beyond the appearances of things. They pray because they are perplexed, disillusioned, frightened, because the way of the world and of religion itself has become too sterile to endure, because, to use Péguy's image, the dovetailing of the temporal and the eternal has become untrue and faulty. The very completeness of the Church's provision for all aspects of men's lives described from one fixed point, provoked a further hunger. Men and women turned, not in any way doubting or rejecting the creed, the practice, the discipline of the Church, to grasp for themselves the reality that these forms expressed, and they turned with a new intensity to prayer to find an answer. There is a wide variety of approach among them. From Eckhart to St John of the Cross, from Julian of Norwich to St Teresa, from Gerhard Groote to St Thomas à Kempis, there runs a thread of passionate desire to seek a truly singular engagement, a genuinely personal relationship with God, to know the Passion of Christ in the simplest and most direct way, to have mind and heart wholly occupied with living openly towards God. It does not greatly matter whether they seek Him in the quiet daily work of the *béguines* or the Brethren of the Common Life or in the strenuous mystical exercises of the reformed or newly founded religious orders. They are seeking to say Yes to God from depths hitherto unexplored. Their praying takes on the character of exodus from the known accepted world, though they cherish whatever in it assists devotion to Him they seek. Profoundly committed to their search, they are explorers every bit as adventurous as Columbus and Da Gama. New dimensions of human consciousness that have lain unvisited as yet, new perceptions of the eternal order clothed in time, are apprehended in their praying and compel them to find new words to describe the journey of the soul.

Exploration, geographical and spiritual, exposes men and women to new ordeals, and their praying reflects their attempts to meet them. Such souls must face with courage the loss of all the guide-lines of familiar features. They must accept the need to let go the things in which they have trusted and face the outlines of a strange benumbing terrifying world. The time-lag between the advent of such new conditions of life and men's awareness of their implications is for very many long and awkwardly productive of unease of mind. The few, like Pascal, who see clearly the nature of this new strange world and feel a loneliness that makes them shudder, begin to work out for themselves in prayer a way of living in it, very much as the first moon-walkers centuries later had to find ways of planting their feet. Because Pascal is, in a very real sense, the first modern man, his *Pensées*, though they refer but little to praying, are the first projected Grammar of Assent of the modern world. They search for the Yes to God that is possible in such a world that is beginning to be disclosed. Henceforward, Pascal sees, men must learn to live with uncertainty, must make their bet of faith, must face the eternal silence, must play out the play of eternal life, with no other assurance of what it is all about than what they may learn from Jesus Christ. New pain has entered man's world. Passion must plumb new depths, and men must pray to affirm their faith in the Hidden God, in God who has taken manhood in to Himself, in God whose Son's Passion proclaims for ever the mystery of existence. Men must pray because only so can they learn to live and grow to their true stature in a world like this which will for ever disclose more questions than answers, in which their freedom will for ever be the trial of their faith, in which the dimensions of moral and mental pain take on quite new proportions.

We are living a little more fully today in the world that Pascal saw at hand. Its pressures have steadily grown. Disquiet and unease combined with a loss of religious faith have put into question the practice of prayer as never before. Men ask for help to set about praying almost as deliberately as they abandon the traditional devotional life of the Church. Very many let prayer go altogether. The difficulty lies not in the often complained-of distractions or shortage of time or lack of concern but in the nature of prayer itself. The questioners ask how praying relates to living, not simply to assure themselves that it can be known to have a 'practical' character, but because they seek some unity or coherence in their lives. They are willing to go apart to pray but they want their praying to grasp all things that this tumultuous world and their no less tumultuous selves confront them with. They want to know how to live with contradictions, and how prayer can deal with fragmented lives.

'I just can't take any more' must be one of the most repeated phrases of our sick society today. Events and problems hammer away at our consciousness and so far exceed our grasp as to suggest, not Browning's Heaven, but Hell on earth. They reduce men to excluding, suppressing and ignoring things in themselves and others and in their world which they can find no way to accept and live with. Too many questions waylay the modern man. Too many of his institutions appear to by-pass the issues which assail his confidence. The search for satisfying engagement goes on at every level. Estranged and alienated man tries desperately to speak to others. Is there another that he can speak to? It is from this angle that Maurice Nédoncelle in his book *The Nature and Use of Prayer* comes to speak of it, putting all the emphasis upon communication between man and man, and between man and God, and refusing to separate the two. Because 'I can't take any more', I turn to you, the other person and you, the ultimate Other, 'you whoever you are' in Walt Whitman's much repeated phrase, 'You whom in faith I must seek out, You to whom all flesh must come.' I cry out to you to resist the intolerable focusing of all things upon this 'I', seduced into supposing that it could live as 'I myself alone', and finding such existence a nauseating deceit.

All praying, whether in ecstasies of joy or agonies of pain, and these are never far apart, begins with such a cry. We cry out like men who take soundings of the deeps beneath us and within. Every man who prays is another Mark Twain endeavouring to discover in himself, in the texture of common life and in his faith in

God what answers with a yes that enables him to live. The christian faith declares, and submits itself to human experience for its own confirmation, that the Yes has been already spoken to mankind in Jesus Christ and that the mystery of human life is most perfectly expressed in the image of the Word made flesh, a flesh that ever seeks to communicate its unconscious wisdom and love by shaping relationships, symbols, images, forms of speech to give utterance to it. We pray to participate in that communication. To say that the Holy Spirit ceaselessly 'prays' is to describe that working of the Divine that seeks to raise this relatedness of creatures to a joyful conscious coherent whole, to an awareness of its fulfilment in God. Prayer in response to this has come far from that reflection on the epic of the nation's history which figured so largely in more primitive praying but it has not disowned its past. It has rather extended and deepened human awareness of the creation itself in travail with the children of God, and of mankind in travail with the life of the Kingdom coming upon earth. We pray as persons in process of discovering what this means. We must needs pray if we are to become and to continue to be persons at all. For that reason, our future as mankind will be decided by our prayer.

Such participation in the prayer we speak of means finding ourselves somewhere between living in a runaway world and running away from life. It is what Thomas Merton was to speak of in terms of contemplation in a world of action, and which led him to require the monastic life of today to be not only contemplative but prophetic. He was asking that those who chose this way of life with its prior claims of solitude, silence and prayer should also try to share something of what they had found of the Mystery of Christ with others, and themselves learn to be as open as possible to the problems of the contemporary world. He wanted their houses to be such centres of prayer as would assist men, whether christian or not, to face together the great problems of the spiritual integration of mankind, as would enable them to learn from each other what the various traditions had to offer, to discover what the embracing of all mankind must mean in terms of the spiritual life. Such a plea might well seem to make too heavy demands upon men and women already extended to the uttermost by their efforts to maintain in the setting of the modern world a life of prayer, but Merton's appeal was shaped by a growing awareness of a world-wide stirring of spirituality towards that end. He felt the sharp goad of the Spirit's importunity combined with human necessity. Generations of churchgoers may well have sung 'We perish if we cease from prayer' without thinking very deeply whether they quite understood what that meant. What the twentieth century had done was to interpret it with stark simplicity and compel men of many faiths to pay increasing regard for what might be called the futurity of prayer. It was a task to be undertaken on behalf of the whole world and it could rightly be expected to draw to itself all those who were becoming aware of its significance. When Lewis Mumford, in his book *The Pentagon of Power*, advised men and women to make such quiet acts of withdrawal, abstention and disengagement from the power-worship of contemporary society, he was describing a familiar feature of the contemplative life, now taking on a quite new relevance to the world of men, and itself needing to be newly discerned by those who came to it.

It is this which constitutes so great a part of the engagement which our Yes to God today must require of us. Something at least of what is involved could be learned from looking again at the best of what had been done hitherto. The practice of a man like von Hügel was there to be seen. For him, it meant keeping very deliberately to certain everyday simple things: saying the prayers of his Church daily, visiting the Blessed Sacrament, making his confession, receiving Communion and being available to help people as generously at all times as he could. It meant further a pondering upon, a wrestling with, the whole range of human activities, cultural, scientific and historical that he was acquainted with, searching in all of them for ultimate significance, searching in such a way that they yielded realities to fire the soul, move the will, enlighten the mind and sanctify the body, so that here and now a man might live as fully as possible in the presence of God, with his face turned in the direction of the on-going journey of God's people. The criticism made of it has been that, for all its sincerity and intelligence, it was the way of a leisured financially secure and cultured life, a life from which the vast majority of men and women have been excluded. The criticism is hard and just. So much of what we have associated with the spiritual life has been attached to the gracious living that few could aspire to. There is something offensive and ludicrous in talking about being quiet and still before God to people who live in homes which night and day reverberate with the sounds of rivet-

34

ing, machining, hammering and passing traffic, in which men on shift work, babies and school-children crowd into a couple of rooms, and where the fight against dirt and squalor is a lost battle. Nor are the newly created housing estates, the blocks of flats and the satellite towns which represent a vast step forward in basic conditions the provision of anything more than an opportunity to face the task of what might be called 'rehousing the spirit of modern man'. At the moment, to an extent before undreamt of, this spirit is in a wilderness. To forget this is to surround spirituality with an atmosphere of falsehood and to lose sight of the most elementary task of our prayer for others. All that we dare to pray must be securely tied to that haunting Biblical question, 'Where is your brother? Why have you not brought him?' It is the spiritual homelessness of the vast mass of urbanised mankind that must set the agenda of our praying today.

It is fair to say that von Hügel was aware of and uneasy about such questions. He believed it to be important to read history deeply to anchor the spiritual life firmly in the hard circumstances of political and economic affairs, and no less important to face the conditions of miners and workers in factories and mills. He did not pretend that he knew how the real and tremendous things of adoration and celebration were to get flesh for themselves in this industrialised life. That they must do so, that christian spirituality must find a way of enabling them to do so, he did not doubt, but he was well aware as were the more sensitive of his contemporaries that the pace of change in society outstripped the awkward efforts of the Church to engage itself with the conditions. The Yes to God passed more and more into default. Carlyle had complained as he looked at the Hero as Priest, at the man whose job it was to discern and speak the truth about life lived by the men of his time, that he seemed to have wandered very sadly from the point. Praying, as von Hügel understood it, was trying to keep to the point in circumstances where everything conspired to hide it or drive those who sought it off their course. The point was the fact of the Incarnation. The question it asked of men was and ever would be the same: is the life of mankind such as honours God who has taken our flesh? The continuing task of prayer was to keep the attention of men upon that question, for it was this that the Yes to God must properly answer.

The stirrings of attention to such things that came to be called the Social Gospel in the nineteenth century and the obdurate indifference if not hostility of the greater part of the Church to such concern were a pitiful comment upon the degree of watchfulness that spirituality must command. It was a state of affairs to be re-emphasised by the efforts of worker-priests and their fate in the twentieth century. It leaves the impression of a church so pinned down under the weight of its institutional involvement with a sick society that it cannot comprehend the question addressed to it, much less summon up and devote its energies to making an answer. Its concordat with the world imprisoned it in just those circumstances that its faith in the Incarnation required it to reject. The cost of disengagement, of liberation, of bringing to an end what at one stage in its history had been picturesquely called 'Babylonish captivity', was real enough in personal terms. 'I am to incarnate, in my turn, the incarnate God.' The cost of such incarnation, held up before men's eyes in the Cross, could not be said to have changed. A spirituality that failed to be explicit about the price to be paid and the actual terms in which it would have to be paid was a fraud. An attempt to by-pass or forget the conditions of human life in which the Incarnate Lord had chosen to dwell was a delusion of spirit. 'Costliness', a word to which von Hügel returned again and again, was thus inseparable from the praying that sought to face the changes in the manner of life that such a faith in the Incarnation called for. John Neville Figgis put it as clearly by saying, 'I have come to see that if christians are to convince the world of their seriousness they must be prepared to live as though they meant the creed which they profess.' It was no new discovery but it needed to be said again. Prayer is concerned with sanctity, and sanctity for those who follow the Incarnate Lord, is that which clothes the man or woman in the course of living out the relationships of joy and pain involved in loving men as brothers in Christ.

It will be our job at a later stage to look at the way in which artists and writers and teachers of all kinds have spoken of this, to treat their work as part of the incarnating of the Word to which in our praying we must be being attentive. Here, one illustration, taken from Iris Murdoch's novel *Bruno's Dream*, may be used. 'Things can't matter much,' she thought, 'because one isn't anything. Yet one loves people. Perhaps this great pain was just her profitless love of Bruno. One isn't anything but one loves people.' Almost all the implications of the christian faith are woven into those words, together with the answer to the question as to why we should pray. The pain is woven inextricably into our lives. It is there in loving, and no less beneath our unloving, unloved, loveless tracts of life. The paradox speaks from it, setting the image of the rejected crucified Christ at the heart of all its experience where, it insists, is a joy that is otherwise not be found. The heartache accompanies the bounding heart. Religious imagery does but extend to an ultimate seriousness those things we have met with already in part, in our origins, in the origins of love and hate, in the discovery of our nothingness, and in the inescapable fact that we love. Whether we can go further, learning to use such intimations of the truth of our being, helping to reshape the conditions of living that we share with others, so that we may grow up into Him in all things is truly the business of prayer. The great epic of deliverance to which Hebrew spirituality clung must be crowned by and issue in a continuing epic of the nurturing of the people of God. We have barely begun to take the question of human nurture where love is most truly expressed as seriously as we have taken man's wars and conquest of power. The pelican in her piety has remained a charming but unconvincing symbol. Prayer needs to probe the sin that has thrust aside its intimations of the meaning of love. Multitudes of men and women have murmured their own versions of John Clare's terrible line, 'I am, yet what I am, none cares or knows'. It sets before us in the clearest terms the task with which our praying is concerned. How much do we care and what does caring mean? It was a theme that Shakespeare mused upon throughout the sequence of his Histories, and brought to an impassioned climax in the 'too little care' wrung from the lips of Lear.

Such prayer must be awake to, must expect and wait upon the revelations that are made in every aspect of our daily life. It must embrace and sing for joy, almost as Teilhard de Chardin does in the Mass on the World, every scrap of the great chronicle of the experience of the Ascent of Man, and face with equal seriousness the challenge to the meaning of life itself that Treblinka and Auschwitz posed. Prayer seeks engagement with such things and refuses to let them fall away unregarded, for all of them are part of the learning process by which men come to know something more of the pain and joy in love. Does this put too much upon frail human beings at prayer? The branch, as Pascal observed, cannot know the tree, but it can, if we shift the figure a little to bring it nearer to the mystery of human life, know the truth of the tree expressed in the branch, the truth of the Christ into whom we ourselves have been engrafted. Such indeed is the task of prayer. It can see and acclaim the truth of the Whole revealed in the part, the truth that is God in the part that is ours. Comment upon it is nowhere more simply and faultlessly made than by Julian of Norwich, saying, 'Love was its meaning . . . we were made through the motherhood of natural love, which love, indeed, has never left us.'

The Yes to it all is hard to make. Every change of circumstance in our personal life as well as in the world we live in, lays on us new demands to keep open in our prayers the way to the meaning of this love. We have to extract from all that happens to us and that demands attention from us, a new confirmation of the faith we hold. Our changing bodies and minds, our changing relations with others and with ourselves, require us to reshape our prayers, or they begin to be less truly the prayers that say Yes to God from the persons we are, the parts that respond to the Whole. Each new stage that we enter upon, whether of marriage or life in a community of a different kind, whether of parenthood, chronic sickness, loss of loved ones and old age, holds out its own infinite possibilities of joy and pain that prayer must embrace. Too often, unwarned and forgetful, we fail to observe the new stages. The bright intention to love is dimmed, the knowledge of being loved is weakened, and the praying that we do gets out of focus with what we are.

Because 'one loves people', because this loving reads into life the meaning we need to live by, we must learn to pray better to honour the love and the life that we know. Men have changed their reasons for praying, their methods of prayer, their styles of life, but their need to pray has remained and grown throughout. Our task is to find what love means in the moment that lies before now. We must mine and refine such love as we can from the tracts of experience we come upon at this time in our lives. 'We have not passed this way heretofore' and we need not be ashamed to confess that we need new help in setting about it. Prayer is our cry for such help, made in pain and joy, a cry to the Other in faith and hope.

3 Prayer and Vision

'These paintings, in my thoughts, represent not the dreams of one people, but of all humanity.'   Marc Chagall.

'Every creative act in science, art or religion, involves a new innocence of perception, liberated from the cataract of accepted beliefs.'   Arthur Koestler.

WE PRAY THEN BECAUSE THERE IS PAIN AND LOVE IN LIFE, because we both suffer and rejoice, because we try to find meaning in it, because we want to share this with another. No doubt a good deal of our praying is shallow and insincere, selfish and immature. What we are as persons speaks for itself in our prayers. It may be the best or the worst that speaks, but what we most deeply need to do is to learn to pray quite honestly as we are, to love and rejoice from the depths of our being. How deep are those depths? Psycho-analysis, had it done nothing else, would have done a work of immense importance here. The most shallow, trivial-minded, apparently characterless person among us carries within himself, it appears, such worlds of passion, hopes and fears, ancestral dreams and twisted purposes, that like the once solid atom, our selves now show themselves to be strange galaxies of particles and energies at work. But that we had bad dreams, we might, like Hamlet, be content with this, or even as Caliban waking might cry to dream again. We have hopes and longings and hungers that aspire to a life transformed. From out the unplumbed depths of this being there is heard at times a voice which is ours yet not ours only. Praying begins with hearing. All prayer attempts to enter those depths below the troubled chaotic self to listen and to respond to a conversation which reveals and summons and helps us to participate in an I-in You, You-in Me relation with the Spirit who gives it life.

This is, of course, how mystical writers speak about it, but most of us are not such people. Our link with such experience is the fact that we love and suffer and exclaim with delight, each in his own perplexed and perplexing way. Great writers manage to put some strands of this experience into words, and we ourselves, when we try to pray, both use their words and search for some of our own. When people ask for help in the matter of praying they want to be helped to do for themselves what their bit of passion and joy craves utterance for. We could speak of it in two ways. One way describes it by saying that prayer is a means to an end, a means of dealing with the things life brings to us and of making some sense of living. The other sees prayer as an end in itself, as if you might use the word to describe what living amounted to in the end. Our praying, poor as it is, is what we have managed to make of life so far. It is also how we are going further. It notices and interprets whatever we have come to know 'of hope and faith and pity and love' which, as a poem of Edwin Muir's reminds us, are better blossoms than Eden ever produced.

Some of this then gets into words and a little of it into the silence that lies beyond them. Most of us find that the help we need must start a long way this side of words. Words all too often get in the way, assume a life of their own, and say things that we don't really know. Of course, the right words help, other people's words help when we're ready to take them, but how do we get to that stage? To think too quickly of prayer as a matter of words can be a most discouraging thing. For that reason alone it would be important to consider how else to approach it. The clue we are given comes out of our human experience too. Before we could talk we could see and touch. Since then no doubt we have learned a very great deal but also forgotten both to see and touch things in a way that kept pace with the deepest needs of our life. We may well be growing more blind and more insensitive to the world we live in, thick-skinned and callous, unseeing and lost. Some therapy sets out to teach men how to touch once more, and our praying, whether as means or end, will be greatly concerned with how we see. Contemplative living is really a matter of learning to see.

Who then shall help us to see and to touch with new innocence of perception? Too often, writing on prayer jumps on too fast to speak of the Vision of God. This sublime mysterious thing has been the object and crown of contemplative living from the earliest days. What better thing could a man desire than to see the fair beauty of the Lord? What more tremendous demand could men hear than to be summoned to seek His Face? So, for the seers and teachers and prophets of Israel, the glory of God, though it threatened to blind their eyes, was the supreme experience of man's life. In Hasidic prayer a man prayed for the sake of the Shekinah and strove to see every bush on fire with God. 'The whole earth is full of His glory' but it needs to be seen. With christian mystics too the seeing seeks the invisible God. But most of us haven't learned to see like that. We can't make out what it means. The words employed to describe it don't help either. We may be impressed by, interested in, even envious of, the visions of others but we want to see for ourselves. We may try to believe that God wants His creatures to see His glory but we also want to know how to begin. Adam, in Milton's brave words, was formed for valour and contemplation, and if Adam, then all of us men. Our problem is that of beginners, and all too often it seems that this matter of contemplation has been treated in too narrow, too rigid, too specialised a religious way that has taken it away from most of the sons of Adam. It is not the fault of the great mystics that this is so, for most of them were too full of common sense to lose sight of created things and our common life. It has been rather a second-rate spirituality, rabbinic in style, timid in vision, prone to the cliché, that has turned this business of seeing towards too limited a range of 'religious' things. From such we must be delivered. It is not the job of spirituality today to turn men and women into second and third rate mystics, but to help them to pray as they can, to pray with the gifts they have got, to be truly themselves when they pray. If this means learning to go back quite humbly to a life prior to words, to learn to be watchful and attentive in a quite new way, then we need the help of those who are accustomed and able to see with unspoiled eyes, who themselves have gone on learning to see when most of us stopped really seeing at all.

Such men are artists, painters, sculptors, potters and the like. What they must do for us is to make us stop and look, notice, marvel and enjoy, see with new-opened eyes the world in which we live. It is no honour to God to ignore His creation, and Péguy was probably right in saying that God was specially pleased with Frenchmen because they saw things in it that most other people missed. When we come on to the poets and writers later, we shall be a little better equipped to follow what they have put into words, and from them recover a use of language that our praying requires, if we have learned a little better to see, and learned from the artists how they themselves have regarded their work. We must persist in trying to see, for, to adapt a description of true faith, a vision that is not open to loss of vision is not true vision at all. Wordsworth, who attached supreme importance to such vision and tried in the *Prelude* to say what it meant, knew only too well how it could vanish. With equal patience we must attempt to follow the always unfinished work of the artist, remembering that Picasso said 'it takes a long time to grow young'. The note of 'not yet' has always to be kept in mind.

How this relates to praying we have now to think. The Bible itself makes much of three important things that link together this business of seeing and a faithful response to God. They are vision, revelation and form. All these have their theological connotations but they have their roots in things seen and pondered upon.

We begin with vision. Again and again in the Bible record a man or a woman simply says, 'I saw'. The moment of seeing is fraught with immensely important things. It arrests this man on his way, turns that one back and bows another to the earth. It changes the course of life, it announces a nation's doom. Men see and shudder, or they see and exult. Sometimes they ask to see more, sometimes they cover their eyes. They see things common as baskets of fruit or things as strange as whirling wheels but what they see is an annunciation, an intimation of the mystery that dwells in the unseen. They speak of it almost in equal terms as investing all things in light or plunging them into the darkness. In the Gospels this matter of seeing is set in the centre of all that Jesus says and does. He is come to open the eyes of the blind; He is also the One whom failure to perceive is the doom of those so marked. Some men implore Him to open their eyes; some He reproaches for claiming to see, and vision may stretch the whole way from seeing men vaguely like so many trees to seeing the Christ transfigured in glory. The story of the man born blind, set out with a wealth of detail by St John, offers endless scope for reflection upon what seeing means. It highlights in parable form the nature of Christ's work, enlightening the eyes of some, confirming the blindness of others, presenting Him, as Simeon had predicted, as a sign to be spoken against and rejected. How much did men see – 'have I been so long with you, and yet!' – how much do we see in the vision we claim to have?

Seeing is no simple matter. Even to claim to see the things of God is a dangerous business, yet, says the Christ, men must be on the watch, prepared to see, looking for the coming of their Lord, awaiting the onset of His Kingdom. If such a note of urgency has largely disappeared from the way in which christians now face the world, if our own expectation lacks this will to vision, may it not be that our weakness in prayer springs from this fact? Watchfulness is inseparable from prayer, is the pre-condition of engagement. In the moments of the great agony in the Garden of Gethsemane, it is the failure of the disciples to remain alert and perceptive that evokes His sad comment on their weakness. How ludicrous too that men should grow to be skilled in forecasting the weather and dull in their vision of God at work in the world. Always the note of warning accompanies the comment upon seeing. Men who gape at eye-taking marvels and misread the signs of the times are in a precarious state.

Notwithstanding all this, He came that men might see. If their eyes at times were holden that they should not know Him, it was nevertheless His will to open their eyes to the reality of life. They must learn to see for themselves and their faith and sight must work together. Only so could they grow into mature discipleship and bear witness to that 'which we have seen with our eyes'. Their testimony, when it came to be made, must be themselves, not as onlookers at the acts of God, but as men being changed by what they had seen. A line in *The Tempest* describing young lovers as having at first sight changed eyes comes as nearly as words can to saying what vision of this kind means. It becomes that absorbed devoted attention to the person so loved, missing no feature or detail of what it observes, that it appears as supplication, the rapt stance of the one who prays.

But the 'vision and the gleam' fade, and the ability to see can be lost or remain inert. The warning that Christ's story gave 'when saw we thee hungry or thirsty or naked?' makes clear that such attention is assailed by interests, fears and passions of quite other kind. Words constantly repeated, assumptions left unexamined, partisan choices recklessly made, blur the impressions that innocence would take. All too easily in the matter of praying the stock phrases of devotional and theological usage crowd out the simpler observation that properly should be its starting-place. There is a silence beyond words towards which all praying moves, but there is also a silence before words, if we can find it, in which we can learn to employ what Wordsworth called 'the observation of affinities', piecing together the sharp fragments of our experience, refusing to be frightened by its discordances and bravely considering its diversity. Only through such attention do the things we see do for our praying what Browning, in a poem like Fra Lippo Lippi, tried to get men to realise:

> *If you get simple beauty and nought else,*
> *You get about the best thing God invents,*
> *That's somewhat. And you'll find the soul you have missed,*
> *Within yourself when you return His thanks.*

The Bible speaks also of revelation, and though the word comes to us overburdened with theological speculation, it carries with it that sense of personal self-disclosure, that implication that men can know and love because they are known and loved, which gives to the Hebrew and christian alike the fundamental basis of faith. It loses its true significance if detached from a faith that anchors it to the mundane life. It suggests that there is a level of perception at which this being known by God takes hold of a man or woman in a way that shapes compulsively their manner of life. The imagery and words of revelation, all too easily construed as a secret message, are less important than the sense of relationship, a conviction that life is of this character and not otherwise. 'Flesh and blood hath not revealed it unto thee, but my Father which is in heaven' is a Yes to the man who has acknowledged, however confusedly, that what he has seen and known of another is a sufficient ground of faith in God. To speak of revelation is an attempt to describe the kind of relationship that the event has disclosed. For creaturely mankind it is as important as creation itself. Men might live appreciative of the created order yet indifferent or even hostile to the personal relationships which revelation insists upon. In a world that knows revelation, circumstances are God. Though the creation itself made manifest His will to create His pleasure in so doing, though God might be conceived of as content to declare His glory in the heavens and the earth alone, not such was the will of the God of Abraham, Isaac and Jacob, of Moses and the prophets. For all His hiddenness which eternally must lie hidden, revelation implies that He seeks to be known through the channel of faith. He summons men to be more than observant. He requires them to respond and to engage themselves, to learn the significance of His purpose and to make it their own. Puzzled as they may be, like the other Judas in the

Upper room, to grasp the meaning of a revelation so declared, they may learn through such a Yes to God that faithful living constitutes the truth that God Himself presents. 'Prayer,' in the words of Franz Rosenzweig, 'is the last thing achieved by revelation.'

There is a further Biblical term to be considered. Creation gave form to that which had been formless and void. Human imagination stops short of the notion of chaos entire, and Milton's 'black, tartareous, cold, infernal dregs, adverse to life' does not help much. We come within reach of the possibilities of knowledge when we gain sense of form. Trembling in our worst moments upon the edge of a Joycean 'chaosmos', discovering for ourselves how with failures in loving, chaos threatens to return, we can none the less lay hold of distinctions of form and by doing so begin to reflect in ourselves what the writer of Genesis means by his comment on God finding things He has made to be good. It is an act charged with self-understanding as much as with awareness of the things so formed. In a description of the drawing of Seurat, John Russell compared his work to something akin to a gesture of love, a way of 'cherishing the form' as he beckoned it forward as if it were some shy creature to be coaxed to come to the light. It was in such sense that Blake sought to express his multiple vision in the form of a man, and to proclaim that to fail to love the human form in heathen, Turk or Jew, was to stand in peril of being engulfed in darkness where chaos is come again.

How closely this bears upon christian spirituality is emphasised by words in the Epistle to the Philippians that endeavour to proclaim the great central feature of the christian faith. The form of God was put off, the form of a man put on! In the form of a crucified felon He was held up to the world. This, declares the christian Gospel, is the form by which He is to be known. It is so disconcerting, so horrifying, so challenging to our sense of form, that we must needs ask ourselves again and again whether we really do see it unfiltered by a host of more mollifying impressions. When men do see this form, even with the most imperfect sight, they wince and exclaim as Peter did when he saw the Lord on his knees beginning to wash the disciples' feet. When men fail to see it they behave as Simon the Pharisee did as he watched the woman who anointed Christ's feet, or as Pilate did when he brought out the flogged prisoner to the crowd. They see no form of beauty that causes them to cry out with delight or sorrow. They revile what they see with contempt. Their eyes gain nothing from the scene to cherish or revere. The form says nothing to them, and that which could, were it perceived, carry men through great uncertainty to some epiphany of wonder, remains in darkness.

With vision, revelation and form, the painter and sculptor are deeply concerned. To see an unfinished statue of Michelangelo is to see form emerging from the stone, to see the beginning of a process through which the artist coaxes the beholder to follow him. He must draw men after him till their feet stand not on the familiar ground of their closed systems of thought, their finished structures for living, their defensive rigidities of taste, but on the ground which is holy where something of the genuine birthright of men may be seen in its purity of form. The artist must do what the New Testament describes as making all things new, enabling men to begin to perceive with the eyes of a child or a lover. 'It would be a bad business for us,' said St Teresa, 'if we could not seek God till we were dead to the world.' It is a bad business for prayer if this is where we propose to begin. Man's fear of nature, of his fellowmen and of himself dies hard, and in the meantime does much to hamper and obstruct his prayer. Only by learning to regard them in a fearless open fashion do men learn to speak with God in the way that the Bible suggests is consonant with the dignity of mankind. Not all that is needed to rid men of fears can be done by artists alone, but theirs is a hugely important job in preparing the way. Theirs is the task of opening men's eyes to the truth of neglected things; theirs the ability to show by contrast what things have gone dead; theirs the chance to recover a vision of things in the world commensurate with their capacity for wonder. It is the eye of van Gogh perceiving a plain chair, a jug of flowers, a wizened old postman, that makes possible a new vision of glory. It is the imagination of Leonardo da Vinci that faces the fears that broke into mind as he studied the natural world and leads him to conquer the fear 'with desire to see whether there were in it any marvellous thing'. It is what men are able to make of their sight of a snowflake, a child's fingers, a tree-trunk, an old man's face that opens up a new possibility of seeing as men saw for the first time such an image as that of the Lamb slain from the foundation of the world. Praying needs that kind of cleansed perception.

Much of the difficulty that most people experience in their efforts to pray springs from a kind of confinement, a too narrow restriction of their attention, of whose character they are hardly aware. Protesting that their faith is concerned with the whole of life, they fail to see that they have grown accustomed to approaching prayer through certain specialised channels. Worship means certain liturgical forms, the exposition of the Word means discourses upon the Scriptures, and the furnishing of churches and places of prayer becomes so traditionally ecclesiastical, that something like an enclave has been created for praying before we begin. Too rarely indeed does a church or cathedral, apart from quite genuine appeals for the relief of the victims of war and disaster, make clear to any beholder how or why it is at all concerned with all aspects of human life. To look into a church is still as it was in Dickens' time like 'looking down the throat of time'. Today we are rather worse off than the men of the Middle Ages for whom the artist carved in stone and wood or painted upon walls and glass the great images of their faith in terms congruent with their outlook upon the world. To the assembled people he could say 'this is your life', the story in which you have a part. Every child today grows up surrounded by a wealth of pictures and models of a quite different world, of life conceived of in quite different ways. These things are there in his home and schools; they are rarely there in the parish church. The world he knows is stocked with marvels; the church he enters is apparently indifferent to them. It becomes itself a quaint museum piece. The adult too, intensely aware of the pressures of change in his life in the world, is met by what looks like an ignoring of any such things. It is one thing to be reminded of the eternal changelessness of God's love for men, it is another to be left perplexed to know how such unchanging love enters our restless unstable dynamic world. Here the house of prayer appears to offer no comment. The great beauty of so many of the buildings and the dated symbolism may serve only to reinforce a sense of nostalgia, to hem in the person endeavouring to pray in a secluded world, while his heart cries out the while for help to live in a more richly disciplined imaginative way in the world outside.

'Nothing else will content its spirituality.' The phrase is Ruskin's, writing in *Modern Painters*, about imagination going to work. Ruskin was too unstable and too narrowly opinionated in matters of religion to be much help in relating art and spirituality, though of all the great Victorians he was the one who most longed to do so. He was keenly alive to the problem, and his influence, coming in the wake of the Gothic revival, was immense.

He had a passionate desire to see and to help others to do so too. He knew that it meant hard work. His failure to do much more than annoy artists and bemuse the great British public left the task he so clearly envisaged unaccomplished and in greater confusion. Nevertheless he points to the problem that mattered – the nature and work of aesthetic reflection and its bearing on spiritual life. He knew, and interior conflict sharpened the knowledge, how much more than sense-perception was involved in the artist's work. The contemplative brooding with something akin to religious fervour he knew by heart. Of that he could always speak. Of what it entailed in terms of what has been called 'unconscious scanning', he had, in pre-Freudian days, too little to help him, and his own incoherence in many wild lectures on art, is indicative of this. Of the artist's work in terms of constructive imagination, the labouring of the man to satisfy himself in his work, the penetration and the conception, Ruskin, in the opinion of Turner, Rossetti and any other artist he 'patronised', knew nothing whatever, though that did not stop him from talking about it. Even so, his conviction that a living spirituality could not ignore or bypass the arts was right, and he could at times give ample evidence of this by pointing to the uglier features of Victorian life. He knew that looking at pictures and sculpture was not an idle diversion or cultural game but a serious delighted response to a demand to be more engaged with life, to be challenged, exalted, stretched and humbled. Ruskin's idea of the job of the artist was like that of the physician described by the writer of Ecclesiasticus: 'The Lord created him too, do not let him leave you, for you need him.' He knew that art was no substitute for prayer but that it was sorely needed to withstand the impoverishment of prayer and to enable men to discern more clearly the great issues in life they must face.

Ruskin rightly sensed the need of the men of his day to be warned against the arrogant sophistication that marked the on-going nineteenth-century life and to be confronted by a determined Yes, which if not recognised as a Yes to God, was none the less on the Lord's side. It came like a tidal wave as the century went on with the work of Cézanne, van Gogh, Renoir and Seurat. It was made in a new and startling language of paint, and offered itself as a parallel to the words of Tolstoy and Dostoevsky, of Kierkegaard and Nietzsche. Painter and writer alike cried, 'Be on the watch', and with hindsight today we may judge how truly their warning was heeded. There is a passage in the sermons of John Neville Figgis that acclaims the post-impressionist painters as fighters, however opposed to the christian Church they might be, on the side of the Spirit. Such insight was rare enough. Watching was not the dominant note of the teaching on prayer. Men were not being called to observe the signs of the times.

The shock-waves of the approaching storms were registered in the work of an artist like Edvard Munch, whose picture *The Scream*, painted in 1893, is a John the Baptist-like cry to an unprepared world, to unmindful minds. It was with Picasso's *Les Demoiselles d'Avignon*, painted in 1907, and since then described as 'a watershed between the old pictorial world and the new', that the prophetic aspect was most nakedly revealed. Men stared, annoyed, affronted and appalled by what appeared to be a quite brutal determination to deform and disfigure the human form. It was felt to be a wanton offensive attack by a man of obviously great powers of sensitive discernment upon the sensibility of his contemporaries. He was not by any means the first and only artist to do such things, but men like Bosch and Grunewald and Goya were in the past, and their imagery could be edged out of too immediate focus. Had Picasso moralised upon the sins of European life in conventional forms his painting might well have been hailed as religious art. Had he painted the Passion of Christ in traditional terms, he might, like Salvador Dali later, have seen his work received with pious enthusiasm. It was precisely the degree to which his work went unperceived in relation to vision and form and revelation in the spirituality of the time that made it so terrible a symbol of failure to watch. Within a decade the unfolding of the implications of this painting burst upon an unready world. Disfigurement on a world-scale set in.

If such symbols and pointers went unregarded, it meant that the praying in day-to-day life was deprived of much that was needed to keep it attuned to the actual conditions of life. The false consciousness that Marx had named went unexamined and unchallenged. What is most needed for prayer that tries to say Yes to God from the actual world of men's lives is help towards seeing and knowing what in fact they are now engaged in doing. It needs often enough to be shocked into a new awareness of the outcome of human behaviour. It needs to be troubled by the sufferings of its victims, by the destruction of its follies. It needs to be awakened from sleep. It is not enough to have pictures of the Passion of

Christ in symbols that no longer disturb and shatter men's complacency and require renewal of faith. We have to see what we've done to the Son of Man before we can say a Yes that is real. We must see how the Cross is planted in our world if we are to find it a symbol of hope and strength and trust for those who live in the world. Only so can it carry men's hearts to the presence of God. The medieval altar-piece could be said to have done so in the terms of the world that men then knew. That world has gone. The place of the altar-piece for the modern man has been taken, as John Berger has said, by the shop-window, for there men see what they desire. Such a world will tend to think of prayer itself as a kind of spiritual shopping with lists prepared and hopes that our orders will be met! Spirituality is not immune to such defilement nor can it be cleansed and renewed unless the eyes of the spirit are opened again. The job of the artist is to help in such awakening of the spirit in man, to free him from the tyranny of the seeming appearances of things.

Such a job must be carried out without cessation. All too quickly the raw wounds can be lost to sight. Treblinka and Auschwitz can be forgotten. The artist must make it clear that our turning away, our readiness to cry, 'We did not know, we do not want to know, we cannot believe that it was so,' avails us nothing in authentic living. Spirituality is not concerned with our defences but with their removal, with presenting us open to God with a broken and contrite heart. Men cannot be contrite about the things they don't see as their own. It is the old problem of coming naked to God, and for that to be truly a Yes of both joy and pain we need the new innocence of perception. The language of the artist, which in this past half-century many have found hard to follow and unwelcome, which has sought to expose the demonic nature of the powers to which modern man has given so great a measure of allegiance, the language of unfamiliar form and unexpected vision, must needs be heard if we are to pray the Passion.

How to make available the needed images and symbols of the Nativity-Passion play? Not one artist alone, not one style of work, not one channel of vision but many are needed. We must learn to be catholic in truth, and begin where we can. In the sculpture of Henry Moore, for example, attention is given to form in a profoundly 'faithful' way. This is not just a matter of whether he carves a Madonna and Child, though at times he has done that too, but rather that in all his work he has searched for life, giving deep attention to the feminine archetype, to the form that endures, bears life, sustains and shields and nurtures and loves. Such a form must lie very close to the foundations of human life and be perceived as such. It must embrace mankind and its children beyond all distinctions of culture and race, must turn our attention from the pursuit of privileged place and possessions and power, must make the play-girl of Hugh Hefner's fantasy world give place to substantial truth. When men have forgotten how to see the human beings before them as anything but material to be used, customers to be satisfied, hands to be employed or vermin to be destroyed, the sculptor must needs go back to a way of seeing that lies very near to the beginnings of life. He must press very deeply towards the roots of the human psyche. In a world that is recklessly spendthrift of humanity, he must discover again the sources of feminine courage and endurance, of strength and tenderness so matched, that a new world can be fashioned from its gifts. The spirituality of the sculptor lies in saying in unmistakeable terms, 'these are the given things of God, these constitute your life'. In a world fargone towards wasteful and callous destruction of natural things, he must claim a new sense of obligation.

Henry Moore and Barbara Hepworth are now elder statesmen of this sculptured new world; their successors have handled new forms and pressed further towards new vision. The task remains one and the same. The world of greater reality is always to seek. In catholic christendom men clung to belief in a world that righted the disasters of this one, and saw all things renewed under God, a world that the icon makes present to those who observe it. For multitudes now throughout the world, the very success of Europe, as Franz Fanon has suggested, has dispersed such hopes. The most ancient cultures and the most distant people have been swept into the shrivelling heat of European achievement. Some, like the Japanese, have opted to play it that way. It is not enough to try to resist. Men must have in their hearts a sense of that form that affirms a quite different knowledge of life and its future, and this the sculptor must give them.

We might learn much from looking again at Leonardo's sketchbooks or pondering upon Rembrandt's drawings. Always the need is to see, to be helped to see. A modern example of this may be given. In the chapel of King's College Hostel in Vincent Square, London, there is a singular object (illustrated on the cover of this book). Where a cross or crucifix might be expected to stand, in the apse behind the altar, a mantrap is set up.* Its arms, of course provide the figure of a cross, while the great spiked circle of steel and the terrible shaft of the barbed spring make clear the intention to entrap and wound a living creature, a victim a man. The familiar outline of the cross has gone, the figure upon it that (dare we say it?) we've grown used to seeing or not seeing there, has vanished. In their place is a simple machine, well-made by a craftsman for the job of entrapping a man like an animal in a snare. We may have forgotten indeed that the Roman cross was just such a machine, much cruder, more lethal than this mantrap here. We may not have begun to think how much more sophisti-cated skilfully designed machines are used as traps and crosses for our fellowmen today. Machines are things that have played a marvellous part in the Ascent of Man. Men have owed so much to them and have taken a pride in their strength, utility and beauty. This mantrap here with its gleaming metal and deadly spring is, in its limited fashion, strong and useful and beautiful too. Like all machines it has had its part in social history. It was devised for and served a purpose approved by a code of social behaviour. It worked no less than the looms and hammers and forges for the possession of wealth. It symbolised and enacted the steps taken to ensure some privileged rights. It hints too at the existence of law-breakers, desperate men who would hazard their limbs and life against the machine for the sake of food. Behind them are women and children. It belongs to the past, to a chapter of human bar-barism and pain now closed. And yet, set there in this deliberate way, it may make us hesitate to think so. Are we quite so sure? Perhaps we know the terrible Kafka story *In the Penal Colony*, and realise that the machine there used to write the sentence of death in the living flesh of the condemned, carefully wiping away the blood and suppressing the cries of the victim in a most ingenious manner, was simply our mantrap or our cross made into a little

* There is a great wealth of symbolism to be explored much further in this work. The Reverend Canon Sydney Evans, Dean of King's College, writing of Mr Louis Osman's work, says, 'Basically his idea is a mantrap and it is a mechanism; the two half-circles with spikes are in fact sprung, and what prevents them from closing is a palm leaf which is fixed back against the structure of the sculpture which is in the form of a cross; and in the centre of the circle is a plain rectangle symbolising human-ity. The thinking, therefore, is that humanity surrounded by all kinds of threats is none the less preserved from total collapse by the presence in the life of the world of the Risen Christ and all that emanates from Him.' What the artist does is to provide us with the opportunity to follow his symbols as they activate imagination in those who will stay long enough to begin to perceive.

more subtle machine. We are all more subtle today, perhaps more adept at stopping our ears and eyes against the sights and sounds that our still more marvellous machines wring from or confront our fellowmen today. Our artist at least has taken a chance, and we may, because of his work, look further and deeper before and while we pray. Whose Body gets caught, whose Blood spills out when the teeth of our machines snap tightly together?

From this single work we can turn to look at the course of an artist throughout his life. In the painting of Francis Bacon there is a prolonged courageous attempt to get us to look at life with a new and more serious moral vision, to see ourselves in the rooms we live in and the clothes we wear with eyes new-opened to the scene. Not the machine now but the figure, the face, the limbs, the posture of the human being are the focal point of observation. Men have painted portraits for centuries now, and revealed a great deal of themselves and their sitters. Bacon has said that portraiture today is an almost impossible task. How much dare the painter show what he sees? How much does the sitter want to be shown? How far can the love and hatred involved in painting be held together? There are portraits of men and women which do not differ greatly from that strange concoction that stares at us from the pages of Shakespeare's First Folio, uniformed men and women, playing a part, putting on a face, concealing the self, dissembling with both themselves and others. The painter and sitter conspired to a bargain, to suggest to the world that such people were stable and healthy and real. Such cheating Bacon rejects. A search for the truth of man's being takes over; the strains, the misgivings, the fears, the interior twists, are all to be faced and revealed.

Such searching to see, such waiting for revelation, such pondering on form, are what we have called the prelude to prayer, the watching without which all prayer grows superficial and inert. In conventional terms, Bacon is not a 'religious' painter, yet few men have done more in recent years to discern more faithfully the pain and joy that invests the soul of modern man, to express the kind of Yes that is made by some men and women whom he paints. The outcome is for many repellent and disturbing. Perhaps we should be more disturbed to find ourselves shocked and repelled, to find how narrowly the lines of our love and compassion are drawn. 'When you love someone,' wrote Péguy, 'you love him as he is,' but that in its turn depends upon taking trouble to face the revealing of what he is. We need to recall the words of Julian of Norwich again: 'I saw his dear face, dry, bloodless and pallid with death . . . for me His passion was shown primarily through his blessed face, and particularly by his lips.' To turn then to Bacon's many portraits and studies is to realise that something infinitely revealing has been done with the lips and other features of the face. He painted in 1944 the work *Three Studies for Figures at the Base of a Crucifixion*. We need to ask what the lips of those involved in a crucifixion would show, and ponder on Bacon's answer. We need to look at the mouth of the nurse caught in the massacre scene that Bacon took over from the film of the Battleship Potemkin. Or we look at the artist's mouth in his own self-portraits, and then again to the *Three Studies for a Crucifixion* (1962) to see the mouth and the parted lips in a welter of bruised flesh. Many have turned away from such a picture dismayed and hurt, but perhaps it was right that they should have done so. What matters for praying is what they do next.

Bacon is so important a painter of our time because his work is expressive of just such scanning in depth that prayer endeavours to do. He does not draw back or turn aside. He does not pretend about what he has seen. 'The particular thing I am trying to do is to make chaos in an isolated area.' The words sound strange, but chaos, the formless void from which God drew His work, stands over against that work and assails it till the end shall come. It is about and within us the whole time, held at bay at infinite cost. What Bacon can help us to see is how the struggle with chaos and old night goes on in the flesh and spirits of humankind, how true was Othello's confession of love as the triumph over the chaos, how purifying, strengthening, re-enkindling is the glimpse we get of love's achievement. Mother Julian's vision saw chaos do all it could to His face, and 'with this sight of the blessed passion, and with my meant vision of the Godhead, I knew that there was strength enough for me and indeed, for every living creature against every fiend of hell and all temptation'. Painting of such a kind faces chaos, as the Face on the Cross faced the darkened world. It does what it can to assert its intention to look for the form that is not overwhelmed by that darkness. It is a great manifesto of something rightly to be called faith.

Our concern is with prayer and spirituality, and we have thought a little about what painters and sculptors are doing, about the kind of Yes that their work embodies. 'Do you really mean,' asks one, 'that as part of our preparation to pray we should make it our business to go when we can and look at such works of art? Are they really so important to our spiritual life as that?' The answer is yes. Men and women once trod out long journeys to visit the holy places to deepen their hold on the things of faith. We can do no less but perhaps will do it in different ways. A holy place is one where some revealing of the love and goodness of God takes place, where we come to see and ponder on that which is shown. We may not find this perhaps as much as our ancestors did in shrines and churches, in tombs of the saints and holy wells, but in schools and places of work, in hospitals, homes and art-galleries too! We shall find the revealing not simply in so-called religious works, but in whatever opens our eyes to perceive with new joy and pain the truth of the life that is ours. It is not to be expected that the perception will come easily or quickly. Eye-opening to such depths is a life-long process and a costly one. It involves putting ourselves to school with those who can help us to gain that new innocence of perception. Paul Klee described himself as living a little nearer to the heart of creation than others managed to do, with the unborn as much as with the dead. It is the artist's function to help us to come a bit nearer, to draw near with faith, to the Creator's heart expressed in His creation. We may or may not be sure that the texture of paint, as Bacon insists, acts directly on our nervous system, but we can take a chance.

Portents of things to come are items for prayer to observe. In a recently opened Museum-Home of Marc Chagall's work in Nice, the desire of a lifetime has been fulfilled. His painting, etching, tapestry and glass have been given a home in which to declare the great Biblical message as he divined it to be. The aim of the scheme was to provide the kind of holy place we have mentioned already. In Chagall's own words, it was to be such a place 'where men can find a certain peace, a certain spirituality, a religiosity, a sense of life', such as the artistry of one man could interpret and make available for others. Chagall thought in such terms, of young and old of every nation seeking in such a house the vision of love embodied in life, the form of the perfect beauty to which our hearts are drawn. A house of prayer for all nations? That will depend on the seeing it helps. His dream, at least, is a gift to mankind.

4 Spirituality and the Poetic

'Why is the Bible more entertaining and instructive than any other book?'   William Blake, *Letter to Dr. Trusler*.

'I thank you, God, for this most amazing day; for the leaping greenly of the trees and a blue dream of sky; and for everything which is natural, which is infinite, which is Yes.'

e . e. cummings, *Poems*.

WILLIAM BLAKE, ARTIST AND POET, FINDS NO PLACE AS yet among those commemorated in our churches as prophets and teachers and lights of the world in their several generations. But neither do Shakespeare and Milton, Keats or Wordsworth; nor are the great novelists remembered for glorifying God or helping mankind. Our notion of saints and confessors is strangely narrow. Our spiritual life is the poorer for it. The absence of any such names points to a disastrous split in our thinking about our life towards God, in our praise of God for His gifts to men, in our use of resources towards answering Yes. It is true that today in our churches there is much more chance of hearing a poem read, songs sung and plays performed than has been possible in the past. Perhaps the movement to overcome that split has got on its way at last. It is none the less true that our spirituality has hardly yet touched upon the great mountain peaks of poetry in its exploration of the way we call Christ.

It is important that we should see this matter clearly. It is not the use of gems from Tennyson or Whittier that we ask for as adjuncts to the Psalms, or selections from Wordsworth to be recommended as spiritual reading. It is rather that, as an integral part of our spirituality, we should take poetry and indeed all literature seriously. Poets themselves have had no doubts about the essential truth-seeking holiness of their work, whether they were so-called religious poets or not. The great Romantic poets, Blake, Coleridge, Wordsworth, Shelley and Keats, deserve to be seen as heading a resistance movement against the dehumanisation of mankind, against the despiritualisation which so many of the factors in their contemporary society threatened to bring about. Theirs is a great wave of warning and protest against the ravishment of men's bodies and souls, an impassioned contention for and on behalf of human dignity. That they were themselves estranged from the life of the churches to so great an extent is but one sorry aspect of the tragic impoverishment of the spirituality of their time.

To take poetry seriously in the life prior-to-prayer we have to get clear in our minds what poetry is trying to do, what any particular poet is doing and why what is done is important to human beings. Despite the reputation accorded to great poets, to regard their work as of genuine importance in the life of mankind today, to suggest that without a knowledge of it we were in any real sense a deprived people, would still be thought to be odd. The uses of poetry, like the uses of literacy, are open to question for many. Poetry indeed, suffers on two accounts. In the hard-headed world of practical matters where the use of words is related to making statements of information, and at its best as it approaches the language of ciphers or mathematics, the poet's usage must seem to be diffuse, fantastic, aimless and obscure, perhaps no better than a 'mental rattle' as Peacock called it, fit only for the infantile stages of society. In the world of religious beliefs, on the other hand, the poet may be thought to be making statements which rival or contend with those that are made in the exposition of a faith, to be trespassing on the ground of those whose job it is to define and proclaim that faith. Such guardians would be not too pleased to observe that Matthew Arnold for one had already decided that the future in such matters lay with the poets. 'There is not a creed,' he wrote, 'which is not shaken, not an accredited dogma which is not shown to be questionable, not a received tradition which does not threaten to dissolve. Our religion has materialised itself in the fact, in the supposed fact; it has attached its emotion to the fact, and now the fact is failing it. But for poetry the idea is everything.' Arnold's words, however true about the shaking of creeds, were not the best exposition of either religion or poetry but his presentiment that the society that lay ahead would need all the help that poets could give it was nearer the truth. What was most needed was a recognition that the poets were not making claims for belief in statements they made as if they were either ideas or statements of fact, but doing a quite different thing in alerting their readers to things to be noticed and faced and pondered upon, in making them sensitive to wider ranges of human experience, in enabling them to order in greater coherence that extended consciousness they are becoming possessed of, in making them, in sum, more preparedly alive to be human beings. Before ever a Yes to God can be made the creature must come alive to the moment and the circumstances and the implications that have to be faced. What poetry does is to awaken a man or woman to the moment, to shape the preparedness from which the response can be made. Spirituality is not simply a widening of the consciousness as some enthusiasts for drug-cultures have suggested, or an increasing of the sensitiveness of human beings, but the employment of all that we have of sensitive awareness and rich consciousness in acts of faithful living. The prayer that we make is the focusing of that effort. What poets can do, and what we need them to do, is to help us to be more adequately prepared in the persons we are for that engagement of ourselves with God.

Poets do this work with words, with words so chosen and ordered, that our learning to read them permits us to share in a more extended, profound and rich awareness of life itself. We read poetry not to stock our minds with the experiences of other men but to be better able to distil the truest experience from the events and happenings of our own life. Where the poetry 'gets across', we are enabled to share more deeply in the human response of living. Great poetry is that which does this in a more inclusive profounder way than the minor poetry which springs from and has its bearing upon a more limited aspect of experience. The greatest poetry, the most inclusive ordered presentation of a man's reading of life, makes possible to us profounder engagement of ourselves in reply. Clearly it matters much to our spiritual life to be open to such communication, to be helped to distinguish between what is valuable or perverse or foolish. The field of consciousness that is not being stocked with what great poets have said and are saying is likely to be at the mercy of a multitude of such users of words as aim at exciting quite other responses. A narrowed doctrinaire rigid outlook or a delusive corrupting fantasy world may well be the things we are left with, and our chances of sharing more deeply and richly in life and prayer are withheld or checked.

The work that the poet does has probably not been better

described than by Coleridge in his reflections upon the power of imagination in *Biographia Literaria* and we might very well honour his teaching in these days by learning to find place among the gifts of the Spirit for 'that synthetic and magical power to which I would exclusively appropriate the name of imagination'. Or we might equally well recall that Blake in the address 'to the Christians' in the poem *Jerusalem* insisted that the Gospel itself was 'the liberty both of body and mind to exercise the divine arts of imagination'. The appeal by Harvey Cox in the *Feast of Fools* for more exuberant playful celebration of the mystery of the faith unfortunately chose to ignore the poets and used the word fantasy to describe this power. But even possessed of such a word as imagination, we have far to go to make our case. There are many who ask what Christ has to do with Apollo or poetry with prayer. To be told that we desperately need the poet to come to our aid in shaping a relevant spirituality still strikes the majority of christians as a little odd. Hymn writers possibly, with their incredibly bad verses, but hardly poets. It is not yet a conception of the ministry that we are ready to welcome. Yet John Henry Newman, whom no one could suppose to be anything but a realist in matters of religion, said boldly in an 'Essay on Poetry' in 1829, 'With christians, a poetical view of things is a duty.' We pause upon that word duty. He did not say something desirable or pleasant or even helpful. He said and meant duty. Nearly twenty years later in an 'Essay on Keble', he praised his subject for making the Church of England 'poetical'. That we may find still harder to take!

That Newman had learned much from Coleridge is fairly clear. Both men were acutely aware of the impact upon the culture of Western Europe of the revolutionary changes taking place around them. Newman was writing in the aftermath of the French Revolution, in the midst of the industrialisation of Britain, and in the current of intellectual questioning that followed and extended the Enlightenment. It was a world beginning to boast that it did not need the hypothesis of God, the world of *Vanity Fair*, the world self-consciously prepared to put its trust in increasing technological facilities. Newman was well aware that only a change of similar proportions in the way men set about their life towards God could enable them to sustain a life of faith in such new conditions. Like Kubla Khan, he heard in the rising tumult voices prophesying much greater conflict, and he sought to make clear how spirituality depended for its resources upon a realistic appraisal of the changed conditions and a language to express their significance. Men must be able to speak with each other as heart speaketh to heart as part of their speaking to God. A new language had to be learned and poetry had to teach it. It is this perception of the importance of poetry to the spiritual life that appears in his word duty. Without such language men could not but be estranged from each other, from nature, from themselves and God. The words in their mouths would increasingly be a deceit, a lie to the user and to those to whom they were spoken, an ideological device such as Marx in the *Philosophical MSS.* would speak of.

Duty or not, the plea went largely unmarked. Great poets came and continued to write, but the forms of worship, the language of prayer, the self-knowledge of faith, the relations of churches went on unaffected by them. The split became even wider. The poet most passionately concerned, William Blake, was ignored and almost forgotten; the devotees of Wordsworth, Shelley and Browning were moved to set up quasi-religious societies. The burst of energy that renewed devotion in both Evangelical and Catholic traditions in the nineteenth century neither faced with serious inquiry the changes going on in the world brought about by technology and science nor paid great attention to what poets or novelists had to say save where a so-called religious theme was dealt with. From time to time there were sounds of alarm. *Essays and Reviews, Tracts for the Times, The Nemesis of Faith, Robert Elsmere*, together with the work of Arnold, Maurice and a great company of scholars drew attention to the need to relate the message of the Gospel to the changing conditions of men's lives, but revivals tended to be atavistic in thought and christian enterprise a series of relief expeditions to succour the more obvious victims of industrialised urban life. A spirituality that imaginatively grasped the implications of the age was not forthcoming. There was little to show that churchmen realised what compulsory education, cheap newspapers, greater travelling facilities, new industries and new entertainment would do for the outlook of the mass of the people. They had been warned a century before. In the postscript to *Clarissa*, Richardson had modestly observed that 'when the pulpit fails, other expedients are necessary', and that he himself had resolved, no doubt with a fairly clear impression as to how far the pulpit was in his own day failing, 'to steal in the great doctrines of christianity under the guise of a fashionable amusement'. A temporary revival of the power of the pulpit obscured the full force of this perception. What men did not see was the coming of days when the process of 'stealing in' all kinds of doctrines would pass to a great extent into the hands of novelists and poets, essayists, reviewers and newspaper writers who had other concerns than that of the christian faith.

The re-discovery of Blake as a great poet, not only by the enthusiasts of the Counter-Culture, but by great numbers of men and women hungering for spiritual reality, must be counted among the significant events of our time, even though we are still at the beginning of appreciation of the nature of his work. What Blake believed, said, wrote and lived was that there was given to man a power called imagination by which he was enabled to perceive and respond to the truth and glory of God. True religion was the exercise of imagination for by it men could perceive 'the infinite in everything', be released from their imprisonment to the sensual and to reason, be redeemed to a knowledge of God through the Yes that they made to the divine-human in Jesus Christ, Himself the Divine Imagination.

Blake saw the life of the poet and artist as that of response to inspiration. He believed that all men were called to make their own Yes to such breath of the Spirit. They had to learn how to respond to it not in an intermittent occasional fashion, not in a generalised way through organised channels, but through every scrap of their work, every personal encounter, every moment's employment of life. The wind of the Spirit blew without ceasing. In dreams, in visions, in unhindered perceiving, men were open to God and free to embody in their own lives the Divine. Blake lived 'eternity in an hour' and saw the infinite in the minute particulars of every form, knew himself to be the inheritor of all things, and sang with pure joy for his participation in them. To speak of him as a mystic, as if to allow him a private channel of spirituality, is to mistake his whole being and work. Blake was alone yet not alone both because he lived fully in the harsh social world of his day and shared in its pains and its joys, and because he lived equally joyfully and painfully in converse with the spiritual world, with the prophets and saints and the Spirit of God. Few men have been more 'engaged' with God in the whole substance of their daily life, few more transparently aware of the Passion. Jerusalem which was his image of the life of mankind on earth set free to be the consummate glory of the incarnate Spirit was to be worked for through every channel of human endeavour. 'Let every christian, as much as in him lies, engage himself, openly and publicly before all the world, in some mental pursuit for the building up of Jerusalem.' With no less clarity Blake spoke of the twofold aspects of Passion.

> Joy and woe are woven fine,
> A clothing for the soul divine; . . .
> Man was made for joy and woe;
> And, when this we rightly know,
> Safely through the world we go.

It is tempting to reduce acquaintance with Blake's work to the choice of *Proverbs of Heaven and Hell*, to quotable striking phrases, and not to engage ourselves in the mental fight, so often carelessly sung about, in even endeavouring to understand the great body of his work. Blake was shaping a new language to express a conception of human life, of incarnate love, of the triumph of Christ, of body and spirit made one flesh, for which there were no adequate images in the minds of men in his time. Such imagery has to be new-made over and over again. Only so can the old imagery be reborn, only so can the Scriptures and the spiritual experiences of men of other generations become present truth and quickening words. Blake found men using the Bible in the very way that Christ had deplored, because they had ceased to learn to speak in the Spirit in their own tongues. They were as men who laboriously learned a dead language and made it the tomb of the Spirit. The words they used were a mockery of their efforts, yet no one laughed. The demand Blake makes is so great that our spirituality has not yet caught up with him. His prophetic writings have not passed into and become a living part of our spiritual perception. 'I really am sorry,' Blake wrote to Dr Trusler, 'that you are fall'n out with the spiritual world,' and the words are still painfully apt. We have fallen out with the ongoing of the Spirit in our world. We act and speak as if it were a world into which God has to be introduced, in which Christ has to be taken to people, in which spirituality is a private adventure, in which we wonder how the Bible can be read as a pertinent book. Blake found the Bible the most instructive of all books because it set out in those minute particulars that he always wrestled to lay hold of the images of the three ages of man's history: the age of innocence which ended with Adam, the age of experience in the Old Testament, and the age of the new man begun in Jesus Christ. He saw how each age presented itself to men in their several lives, and he shuddered to see how innocence was betrayed, experience turned to bondage, and the life of the Spirit excluded. 'It is eternal winter there,' he wrote, and had he not himself lived in the light of the quickening Spirit he could not have borne the miseries of that rejection nor continued to fight for the 'mercy, pity, love and peace' in which his soul rejoiced.

'My business is to create.' No words Blake ever used were more precise in respect of his intention and of the way in which he looked at life. For him the Creation was a continuing thing in which as ministers of Christ all men and women were called to do their work, to fashion a new body of imaginative response, a clothing for the soul divine. Prayer was the focusing of the whole attention on such creative action. All the necessary materials were made available through the senses. Single vision perceived no more; twofold vision subjected them to intellectual analysis, the threefold made them the object of love, but it was the four-fold vision alone, the work of the imagination, which enabled men to perceive the infinite in all things and thus come to the vision of God. For the poet it was the special task to awaken the spirit in man to see all things in the light of their eternal reality, to draw them into the conversation in which, as in his own poem 'Jerusalem',

> they conversed together in visionary forms dramatic which bright
> Redounded from their tongues in thunderous majesty.

Blake read the Bible as part of this conversation, saw forgiveness as the great warrant of its continuance, contraries as the condition of movement, energy as the source of delight, and poetry as the vehicle of its expression. His vision of Christ, as he well knew, was clean contrary to that which was so widely presented to men's eyes, yet to the end of his days he never ceased to sing aloud of it.

Blake's imagery may be said, in Caroline Spurgeon's words, to hold 'within itself the very secret of the universe'. Writing of Shakespeare's images, she observed that in such usage lay a revelation, largely unconscious, given at a moment of heightened feeling, both of what the poet had seen and stored up and ignored and forgotten. What the poet is doing is to make available the means of cleansed perception that enabled the man or woman so

aided to see with new intensity of vision 'into the life of things.'
It was such a conception of the poet's task that Wordsworth made
his own, and two centuries after his birth we have special reason
in endeavouring to make a realistic Yes to God to have his contribution to spirituality very much in mind. It is not difficult to be
scornful of 'picking daffodils with Auntie Wordsworth' and very
easy indeed to grow impatient with his theories about poetic
diction and his choice of subjects in peasant life. But there is also
in his best work that constant indication of an approach to the
natural world which makes it resonant with accents of the eternal.
Since his day men have looked at and written about nature with
keener eyes than Wordsworth's, and this is a great gain and a
tribute to poets who turned men's attention to the earth. Wordsworth himself was fundamentally concerned with something
other, with the spiritual energy that had given birth to rocks and
trees and clouds and rivers, in the presence of which the human
spirit might recover a purity and generosity which otherwise was
eaten away with meanness and triviality. He is essentially a poet of
baptism, of being washed clean, of simplicity restored and dignity
revealed, of the ordinariness of living that the bread and wine of
the eucharist are part of and through which the infinite movements of the eternal spirit are made known. Wordsworth's imagery
is always in movement towards silence, always passing through
things heard and seen in their most majestic, austere and awe-
inspiring forms to a silent awareness of the eternal.

The testimony of poets to the work of poetry carries its own
diversity in unity, whether like Shelley they speak of 'the interpenetration of a diviner nature through our own', or like Newman
of 'originality energising in the world of beauty'. Wordsworth
had no doubt that the 'more than usual organic sensibility' of the
poet was charismatic, a gift to be used to kindle among men a
more lively awareness of that power from which all that was
truest in their own nature was derived. Saying Yes to God was as
necessary for mankind as turning to the light or breathing was in
the organic world. His own understanding of that necessary response he laboured to express in the Prelude and the still longer
projected works, for like Spenser and Milton he was possessed of
an overmastering desire to put all he had and knew into one
supreme work, an act of worship devoted to God Himself. It
was not nature-worship, as Blake suspected, nor semi-atheism as
Coleridge was moved to complain of, and it was very far from

wanting, in his early days at least, to do as Keble or Herbert did, to put the articles of the christian faith into verse. Had Wordsworth grown up in the tradition of a generous catholicism his Yes to God would have been a Teilhardian poem, a great act of contemplation at once profound in its scope and lyrical in its utterance. As it was, with little to help him from the great inheritance of christian devotion, and stopping far short of Shelley's indignant defiance of ecclesiastical corruption and blindness, he shaped his own responsive Yes to that 'Being spread o'er all that moves and all that seemeth still' as to a revelation that commanded his whole self-giving. It was done at a time when men were about to begin the rape of the earth with a brutality not hitherto known, when cities and villages alike were about to be made the great wens or festering sores that Cobbett so loathed, when a ruthless conquest of nature would make clear its own absence of respect for any God or gods but mammon.

The Wordsworthian legacy for spirituality is a more detailed Benedicite, the unpacking and rejoicing over and delighting in the infinite variety of things seen in the world of nature, which fills out the perpetual benediction that he himself described as the fruit of his own contemplation. If it lacks much that relates it overtly to Christ, if it is open to the criticism of turning away from 'half of human fate', it is nevertheless nearer to the starting place of the spiritual pilgrimage of great multitudes of men and women today than the Christ of ecclesiastical tradition. Wordsworth began his own journey a long way further back, just as many are minded to do today. His own sense of engagement and of passion were no less revolutionary for being expressed in quiet withdrawal and patient attention to commonplace things. He did not reject the ministrations of the Church, even though for a time he found much in them offensive, but he dug deeper in his acquaintance both with nature and human beings to discover for himself a healing power and a sense of wonder. He found them among such as lived

> *By sensible impressions not enthralled,*
> *But by their quickening impulse made more prompt*
> *To hold fit converse with the spiritual world,*
> *And with the generations of mankind*
> *Spread over time, past, present, and to come,*
> *Age after age, till Time shall be no more.*

In such company he endeavoured to speak of the things which lay at the source of life. He knew that men cut adrift from the vision of glory in that natural world were in danger of losing all sense of glory whatever. He also knew something of what was at stake in the crisis of language, realising that the language of poetry like the language of religion could be falsified, and he dreaded the seductions of both. He knew that men skilled in the use of such diction took away the key of knowledge and encouraged a vain chattering about holy things, a state of affairs that many men know today when they long to cry out and protest about too facile employment or words and phrases that pertain to God and His Christ. It was the poet's job to struggle for a return to simpler, authentic, honest usage. His own theory as to how it was to be done, his explanations of this own practice and of the nature of poetry, were not happy, but his instinct was sound. Intimations of the divine demanded a more humbled response, a greater sense of the mystery of common speech to serve the greater mystery of 'the master light of all our seeing'.

But christian spirituality must, between silence and silence, speak and be heard among men. It must move into the cities. 'Why is it,' asked T. E. Hulme, 'that London looks pretty by night?' and his question shows that we have moved a long way from Wordsworth's exclamation at the beauty of the city in morning sunlight. Hulme answered his question by referring to the ordered pattern of lights, the enchanting tracery of illumination, that held and diverted attention from 'the general cindery chaos'. It was, he argued, a brave beautiful almost theatrical display of all that organisation of the world's 'mud and cinders culminating in man and his cities, which in a few moments might return, like the cities of the plain, to chaos and old night'. It was no new reflection for the artist and poet, though Victorian spirituality did not pay any great attention to it. The poets and artists had all along known the high price to be paid for the beauty of form that made known the nature of God, the passionate price for engagement of any such kind. Upon the poets of the Victorian scene it broke with great fury, surging through 'In Memoriam', chilling the poet-pilgrim to the Grande Chartreuse, leaving a wistful questioning and an ironic sigh to the Spirit of the Pities that moved Hardy to poetry. But it was in Browning's work that the conflict with chaos was dramatised in the most personal fashion, anticipating in its imagery of whirlpools of self-questioning the confusion of voices in the consciousness of twentieth-century man.

Browning still suffers from light-hearted quotation of ·lines from 'Pippa Passes' and 'Rabbi Ben Ezra', not because the assertions of the best being yet to be and the fact of God being in His Heaven were not in key with Browning's attempted grasp of things, but because, detached from the rest of his work they tend to falsify his real contribution to spiritual integrity. Browning was quite ready to give great shouts of delighted glee and pleasure, to exult where he could in 'a wonder and a wild desire', and to confess the attraction of the 'gift of eloquence, of language that goes as easy as a glove o'er good and evil', but the truer, more mature side of him wrestled as if the glove simply would not go on without splitting at the seams. The shouts he gives are those of a man who cannot help crying out in wild amazement that somehow, exhausted and bewildered by his effort, he has managed to do it, and that this, true triumph as it is, is but a step towards another more difficult feat.

The real difficulty of making good use of Browning springs from our common desire to have our difficulties named and accounted for as quickly as possible, to have a rough notion of what we're involved in. This 'semantic stutterer', as he has been called, will have none of this. He insists that we look at half a dozen irreconcilable features or listen to a score of contentious voices that he, the poet, is aware of, and of which we have hardly dreamed of until now. The moment he utters them we know them to be authentic voices of our near-chaotic selves set in the world 'where the possible was the improbable and the improbable the inevitable'. We have, by becoming involved in Browning's introspection of others, been pushed a little nearer to self-knowledge. The immediate effect, as often as not, is baffling and the best man, in Browning's estimation, is the man who suffers most in this endless quest for what God intended him to find, who goes through with the passion that such an engagement demands. Whether 'forced to muse the appointed time' like the Jews in 'Holy Cross Day' (How long, O Lord?), or to go on 'because nought else remained to do' like Childe Roland, or to argue the matter out like Saul or Mr Sludge or Bishop Blougram, or to have to listen to all the voices of the people in the Ring and the Book, men embody something more of this otherwise spiritless mud and enable it to become a significant voice in the creation. Browning had an unshakable confidence in the worth of the fragments, the broken bits and pieces of lives that got nowhere, the great company of the lost who stand ranged along the hillsides to watch the latest lost soul blow its defiance to the powers of evil, 'a living frame for one more picture'. Always his imagery seizes upon the apparent failure, the defeated purpose, the inert stuff, and treats it as precious metal to be refined and used again.

So Browning is, if we are ready to use him rightly, a great source of help in the refashioning of prayer. He did two remarkable things. He showed on the one hand that a single event like the sordid crime that lies at the heart of the Ring and the Book can reveal the multiform mystery of human life and the points at which it suddenly discloses 'new depths of the Divine'. He made it equally clear that the poorest coarsest human hand was fit subject to be so studied as to reveal the 'crowning grace', and this, not in any easy fashion but as the outcome of deliberate acts of faith. Browning's imagery is almost always the language of prayer because it sets the object of its perception between men and God and talks about it as of something profoundly important to both. It is the language such as a child, a lover, an artist, would want to use to carry on a conversation. It is serious, excited, joyful, wistful and expectant. It grows breathless with delight and incoherent with perplexity. Always it strives to make clear, whether it deals with people or things or events, that through them 'God stooping shows sufficient of His light for us i'th dark to rise by'. The men and women that Browning writes of are, almost without exception, moved and stirred by the Spirit to turn at some moment towards that light. Not of ourselves but of Him is the quickening act, and the faith that responds.

Hardly any British poet says so much of faith in all its phases, whether it be no more and no less than 'perpetual unbelief kept quiet like the snake neath Michael's foot', with the knowledge that it will never get any easier to keep one's foot there; whether it be the facing of all change in the image of the Christ so that . . .

> *That one Face, far from vanish, rather grows,*
> *It decomposes but to recompose,*
> *Becomes my universe that feels and knows.*

or whether it issues in half-weary but still trustful reference to his Friend

I can simply wish I might refute you,
  Wish my friend would, – by a word, a wink,
  Bid me stop that foolish mouth, – you brute you.
  He keeps absent – why, I cannot think.

Even so the dialogue will go on, and Browning's poetry is directly relevant to all modern spirituality, because, in spite of his own choice of the word monologue to describe so much of it, it is in reality that kind of dialogic encounter that Buber speaks of as the place of the expected theophany. It deals with what is essentially the business of prayer, the responsive Yes that a man must endeavour to make in those moments when the engagement is offered to him, when to be truly himself he must speak the truth in love, when he is presented with the opportunity and the responsibility of framing his reply 'in spirit and in truth'. Browning knew that the eternal Word waited to be embodied in human speech. In such moments all the divine events from the Nativity to the Passion are in our human key re-enacted. The Word may be given no room, may be misunderstood, treated with contempt, entirely rejected, but it is certain that, because of His love, it will not cease to be uttered. It is in this sense that the language of poetry is the serious speech to which all prayer aspires. The poet knows only too well that he himself is failing again and again to speak as he should, now wrestling with unmanageable perceptions, now giving way to the deceptions of easy speech, now intruding a false self-consciousness into the area where openness should prevail. The poet can just as easily get in the way of the movement of the Word as anyone else. He may be all that Shelley said so magnificently about the poet and still betray his calling. None the less, he shares in the forgiveness extended to us all. It is his job to enable words to become bearers of the Word, to permit the Word to take our flesh and dwell among us, to speak the words that hallow all that God has given and man has received, to translate them all into a Yes to God.

5 *Prayer and the World of Men*

'In the Incarnation God has affirmed the world, and affirmed history, and the particularity of history.'
R. Gregor Smith, *The New Man.*

'There can be no radical division between civilization and what belongs to the interior being of man.'
J. Daniélou, *Prayer as a Political Problem.*

IN A WORKERS' EDUCATIONAL ASSOCIATION CLASS OF which I was the tutor many years ago, there was a small elderly woman who interrupted my lecture from time to time by asking 'Who's we?' It was a salutary interjection. I had, no doubt, been saying that 'we do this' or 'we think that', forgetting that it was a very small section of humanity that I was talking about, and that outside that room there were millions of people who were being ignored or forgotten. 'We' were a handful of literate, reasonably clad, reasonably fed, reasonably housed and sufficiently leisured people who were able to meet together to talk about social problems in decent conditions and without fear that we might be raided by the police and taken away for questioning. Only when one began to enumerate such details did it become clear how much we were taking for granted. We knew a little of our own social history, we could look back to harsh and difficult times, but we could have no real conception of what life meant to those who were squatting homeless in the great cities of the world, or to those who were dying of hunger in the famine areas, or to those who were victims or even survivors of the concentration or labour camps. We couldn't for that matter know what it meant to be black, to be refugees, to be terrorised night and day. We could read of such things and see them pictured upon our screens, we could take up their problems as good causes to be worked for and be as generous with time and money as we dared on their behalf, but to get inside the skins of those who lived such lives and know

70

what it meant to be born in that state of life was altogether a different problem.

Do we need to do this? Is it really a matter that touches our present concern for prayer and our over-all faith in Christ? Do we see ourselves and our praying as somewhat apart from this troubled and troublesome world with its vast agenda of problems of every kind, or must we be somehow involved in them all, and if so, how? Or are we an élite, not choosing to be so but chosen, whose job it is to live in the world in an uncompromised way, resisting corruption, maintaining the faith, praying for the people of God but needing for this to keep somewhat apart? Or are we, just because we are christians trying to pray, engaged with the world in a forthright and difficult way that plunges us into these problems and shrinks from none of them to do in that cultural turmoil what faith in the Christ would require? Such simplification of choices before us, however made, could plainly be dangerous too. We are likely to opt for the broader concern for the world, to affirm that the Christ is the Lord of all life, to admit that we anyway live in the world and that we can hardly avoid doing something about it. But what does this mean when it comes to the practice of prayer, and what does it mean for the role of the Church in the world? The choice may be right, but it is only the beginning of a long, difficult and surprising journey, by no means the first of such journeys in which men have lost their way and found their hearts failing them. That is no reason for not attempting it or for turning back, but it does add greatly to the job of being watchful, enduring and hopeful.

A genuine exodus is full of surprises. The kind of engagement in prayer for the life of the world which we contemplate now is bound to be so charged with new versions of old problems and entirely novel difficulties that there may be little to help us in what we have done in the past. We have to learn to go beyond sheer continuity or precedent, to live off the land, to expect to be shown by the Spirit at each stage of the effort what it is that must be attempted now. To 'all things original, spare, strange' we have to be ready to give a welcome. It means learning to let go much in which we have hitherto trusted, attached great importance to and valued rightly at that time. It is no treason to our faith to do so nor is it the easier option. To pray for the world of today is to be immersed in a sea of difficulties. It is also to realise that within the life of the Church, disconcerting as it may prove to be, the waves of change are no less mountainous. Perhaps we have hardly begun to estimate what these changes amount to or demand of us now. We are still too near to Vatican II's addressing itself to the Holy Spirit, too near to the Ecumenical Movement's leaping over walls, too near to a newfound awareness of the spiritualities of Judaism, Islam, Buddhism and other faiths that have come our way, to realise, to be wise about and to be wholly welcoming towards what has been done for us and to us. Less than thirty years ago Teilhard de Chardin wrote that 'there is no present sign anywhere of a faith that is expanding'. He was looking for that kind of christian faith that could, with sensitive understanding of what it was doing, reach forward to embrace the world that lay ahead, a faith in God 'proportionate to the newly discovered immensities of the Universe whose aspect exceeds the present compass of our power of worship', a faith that would enable men to take hold of all the elements of their newly made culture and weave them together to sustain humaner life, and he felt terribly alone.

Today we dare say that the changes have come, that change has come to stay, but we find it no easier to interiorise these changes or to decide what they mean. That grinding of the gears we spoke of earlier is so often the witness to the sense of disruption that is felt as resulting from the changes. Church-people accustomed to routine and inclined to be defensive in their attitude towards the world, aware that they have sunk a good deal of capital of various kinds in their institutions and practice, are not very well equipped to think and pray in nomadic terms. 'To your tents, O Israel' has a fine stimulating sound at times, disengagement may very well be needed to make way for new ventures of faith, but a disciplined learning together of how to do this as part of a fundamental new engagement with God has not been the main concern of our churches hitherto. Our Yes to God, genuine enough no doubt in its perception of His blessings and mercies in the past, is not easily given a new and apparently disproportionate dimension. Yet such is the task of our praying today. It is no bad thing to be reduced to a sense of dependence upon God all over again since the Yes that we most need to make is the Yes of faith. A turning point in life may very well be, as Saul becoming Paul discovered a time of blindness when you have to be willing to be led and taught all over again to see what you have hitherto resisted, an irksome, humiliating, baffling time that threatens to stretch faith to breaking point and oust hope by despair.

We are now concerned with the world. For prayer this means catching up in a quite new way with the meaning of God's affirmation of the world which in theological terms is expressed in the Incarnation of His Son. The world of men is given its meaning by this act of God, by this Yes that He has spoken to it. In the past men have lived in their fragments or portions of territory and culture and history, vain-glorious enough to suppose that theirs was the true life of men, the apex of culture, the service of God, without any need to do more than consult their own well-being. Today a new sense of the world is required. The words that describe it are simultaneity, unity, pluralism, communication, personalism, indicative of the discovery of the need for a unified human life of infinite diversity in expression and concerted purpose to explore and extend its conscious direction of life. The Yes of mankind so far has been largely a yes of existence, a laborious painful attempt to permit human life to continue at all. The Yes of the world of today and tomorrow must be that of deciding what kind of humanity lives on the earth, a Yes that not only embraces mankind as a whole but takes note of the interior 'worlds' of each person within it. That no man lives or dies to himself alone takes on a reality never before in human history faced. It involves no less acceptance of the legacies of past history in terms of recognition and reparation that bespeak a new sense of human responsibility.

In such terms we describe the spirituality for today. Prayer must spell out in detail what this means for every participant in it, must bring home to each person indeed that they are participants in it, and that it is in and through such participation that they make their responsive Yes to God. It means an end to any idea of 'private' as distinct from common prayer, or of prayer as severed from living in the world, or of the life of religion as detached from immediate temporal purpose. It must set before men the task of freeing themselves to engage with each other as persons, to be masters not slaves of their technological-scientific equipment, to be morally responsible towards the future with imagination and humility. Such praying must further enable the Church and the churches to free themselves from too heavily Western-Europeanised and clerical forms and institutions, to be wiser for having had courage to see their mistakes and follies in the past, to be penitent for their pitiful claims to authority, to be ready to shape themselves as communities able to nourish the lives of all people who come into them. Making use of that vision of artists and of imagination such as poets make use of, such prayer must take notice of all that belongs to the social, political and economic life of the world, to the education not only of its children but of all its members, to that personal freedom that gives spiritual space for men and women to grow up in, to that delight and celebration of beauty which says Yes to the glory of God revealed. This is engagement as never before. It will not be attempted or sustained unless men see a little of and care enough about the task assigned to them at this point in time. Teilhard de Chardin spoke of it as the ultra-human. We may just as truly call it the coming of age or growing up of mankind.

Who is sufficient for such things? Does it make the spiritual life too difficult for the ordinary men and women we are to face? How are the quietness, solitude, disengagement from ourselves that have been so important in the practice of prayer in the past to be treated now, how much or little of the traditional forms of spirituality are we to take with us in this task? The fact of insufficiency is plain to see and hard to bear. Paul pleaded it and got his answer. The answer stands today. Divine engagement with the world through Jesus Christ is unimpaired. Divine equipment of His servants is, we believe, as adequate as ever. 'When I sent you forth without scrip or shoes, lacked ye anything?' The question is whether we want to be so engaged. We are not the first of His servants to be appalled by the assignment held out to us. It is very likely that we shall only find the relevant adequate spirituality for this task by way of bankruptcy in what we supposed we had, and by being thrown anew upon the teaching of God's spirit. The saying that it's the poor that help the poor may take on a new application to ourselves. Our newly felt poverty may be our best resource.

The dread of over-complication deserves attention. It is well-known in religious history that men turn the mystery of God into mysteries too hard for others to bear, and a secular form of that mystery-mongering flourishes anywhere in the world. Yet Christ spoke of things revealed to babes and Himself took the risk of being misunderstood. What he sought was not the knowledge of the learned but the honest avowal of men and women of what they had seen and heard. We do not repudiate the work of the experts in theology, philosophy or any such discipline if we nevertheless choose to regard their work as comment upon experience rather than experience itself and pay more attention to the kind of experience that common life in the body of Christ provides.

But the demand goes deeper yet. When we ask what all this means for the practice of prayer we are bound to admit that it shows ill-preparedness and chronic immaturity in church life. Such a notion of prayer has not been in the forefront of the agendas of the great majority of churches, and we must learn the hard way to do better. The changes of the past ten years have brought about a new awareness of the need to pray for world-affairs, and aids to prayer directed to this end are detailed, well-informed and more imaginative than at any time before. But aids of any such kind demand attention to the way they should be used, and this means specially getting clear how we in this particular church or group see ourselves in relation to our immediate neighbours and the world, how much of a piece is our life in the Church, the world and our inner selves. It needs to be seen that in spite of our talk of a Catholic Church we are all very much inclined to live in pockets of our own choosing, and these to a large extent shaped by our social standing. Isolationism goes very deep. A friend of mine once pleaded that the members of the Church he attended might meet together for the simple, if profound purpose of getting to know each other. He was met with the chilly retort, 'Do we want to know each other?' We can live in close proximity with these members of the Body of Christ apparently and be quite unrelated to them.

There can be no movement of prayer towards the concern for the world we have mentioned which does not begin with the particular albeit common needs of men and women everywhere to be treated as persons and neighbours and friends. The Yes to God of a unified world is shaped in the relationships of each locality, in the willingness to embark upon such conversation or communication which allows the personal life of others to grow. Community waits upon such communication. If we choose to deny that basic condition, we must repel the Christ who knocks at our doors and the heavens that overtop our barriers. For Christ Himself, having identified His own mission with that of the prophets before Him, made clear the requirements of true worship and of spiritual health. He insisted that they turned upon the kind of relations that obtained between man and man. He proposed the quite searching test that men should examine whether their brothers had grounds of complaint against them. He recalled that the God of Israel was desirous of mercy and justice in social relations before all kinds of ritual offerings. The prayer that does not take note of such conditions is falling far short of the manner of praying that Jesus commended.

Two questions have to be kept in mind throughout. Do we see what disengagements from the sins of the world are called for before any Yes to God can be realistically made? Do we take it as part of our spirituality now that we seek with unwearying passion to discern what engagement with God in the world of today must mean? Much of the superficiality of our praying stems from the lack of sustained and factual examination of the behaviour of men and nations towards each other. To affirm the particularity of history means taking seriously the details of what is done. The Psalmist was right in his contention that his tears and groans were marked just as Abraham Lincoln was right in insisting that each drop of Negro blood spilt under slavery would have to be atoned for, just as Casement was right in claiming the same for the iniquities done in the Congo. The blood of Abel cannot be hidden from remembrance in quaint stories or forgotten history, for the job of prayer is to bring men to the knowledge of the truth about themselves. Jesus Christ was nowhere more searching in His comment upon false spirituality than in His observation on the facility with which men claimed to be innocent of their fathers' propensity to stone the prophets. It is good that the Church should remember to honour the martyrs, but it is also needful she should remember the victims of her own blind acquiescence in the sins of society and her own cruel lapses of charity. That sense of 'We' will be disastrously complacent and deceptive in both public and hidden prayers if it fails to keep before the minds of those who use it some knowledge of specific sins which witness against us even now. At whose expense do any of us enjoy our affluent society, our health, our food, our education, housing and protection?

Not infrequently we are asked to be on guard against a humanism which limits attention to the well-being of men, and loses sight of the divine. As christians we take the warning to mean that it is possible to lose sight of the true nature of human life by acquiescence in some formula devised for its description. Men can impose upon themselves conceptions that deny their destiny in God, becoming fearful of the freedom that He has offered to them, choosing rather to worship their own political and social institutions, suspecting and persecuting whatever threatens to question them. Christians must out-humanise all that so narrows and denigrates and degrades the human being, sorrowing the more deeply for what has been and even now is done to warp and mutilate this human nature, but holding fast to its true dignity in Christ. Humanisms are deficient in what they deny, not in what they affirm, for no humanism could exalt mankind beyond that which christian faith declares to be the glory of man. Perhaps the most neglected aspect of our praying so far has been a serious grappling with the implications of the doctrine of the Incarnation, for had we done so we could not have dared to neglect, to maltreat, to despise, to abuse, the multitudes of men and women whom He has chosen to make his brothers and sisters. Prayer must be fashioning a Yes to God that works out in the life of the whole world what such a faith entails. In picturesque terms it means seeing not only Moses and Elijah standing with the Christ in glory on the holy mount, but seeing Him in 'the field full of folk' that Langland saw from Malvern Hill and the city crowds that throng the streets today. In other terms it means asking what is to be done for child-welfare, race-relations, sickness and old age, for penal reform and education, for housing and conservation. What is done or not done to the least of these His brethren is the measure of the Yes that is being made. Because He has chosen to take our flesh, we cannot set these things aside and offer to approach Him in a manner that we deem more fitting. Worldliness wins when praying ceases to engage us with the society in which we live, when we become shockproof to the iniquities and cruelties it admits and too timid or careless to seek for redress. The business of prayer is to help us to care for the world as God cares for it.

What then is our capacity for any such Yes as this? We do not, and cannot know it, until the layers of our customary self-protection are penetrated by the light that He Himself throws upon the scene, until the pre-occupations that engross so great a part of our attention in churches are subjected to a more searching critique than we commonly make of them. It would not hurt the christian Church to meet in houses and hired rooms, to stop providing 'services' to meet occasional demands, to overhaul its use of the ministry and its financial resources, to develop a hidden life of far greater passion than its present public custom. 'He casting aside his garment came to Jesus.' A new seriousness in prayer would bring such things into question, recovering from the Bible that note of interrogation that the Yes of the people of God must be subject to. Christians must learn to hear that questioning too in what secular witness has to say about men's history, industry, culture and religion. They must learn to stop asking for a privileged position in society, and even more, stop bargaining with subtle treacheries to God and man to get it. They must learn, up to those unknown limits of capacity, as Bonhoeffer, Hromadka, Delp, Maria Skobtsova and others have taught us, what engagement with the Passion of Christ in the world today, must mean. Wherein have we wearied Him? Wherein have we robbed Him? In what ways have we rejected Him? What Hans Jurgen Schultz called 'conversion to the world' implies and demands more thoroughgoing search for the Christ who is there already, more determined scanning of His features in the form He takes on Himself in this stage of human history. It means perceiving how He is crucified afresh by callous hands and opinionated minds in such a world. Prayer must be enabling men to come awake to such a task, and the change that is called for must out-top the changes going on in the rest of human life. The christian cultural revolution must be much more radical than all others, christian rectification go much deeper. It will not do so, it will not be wanted to do so, until we learn to look afresh at the title-deeds of our faith. There is a curious moment in Trollope's novel *The Warden*, in which in the course of a discussion about the future of Hiram's Hospital somebody suddenly asks 'but did you ever read Hiram's will?' All ancient institutions tend to be taken for granted by those who have grown accustomed to them, and the changes that can convert them into being and doing things quite opposed to their foundation purposes can pass unnoticed, and the heirs read back their own assumptions in place of the unexamined titles.

It is with the Passion of Christ in the world today that we must start in our prayers, with the pain that He in His embracing of the world is condemned to suffer. That means that suffering must be seen and known and not ignored wherever it is.

> *None can usurp this height, returned that shade,*
> *But those to whom the miseries of the world*
> *Are misery, and will not let them rest.*

There have been indubitable gains in the recognition of international and national responsibility for such suffering in the past twenty years, and the danger is that the organisations created to give effect to them should be taken for granted too and cease to be regarded in prayer as points of pain. Built-in shock-absorbers can bring about a condition of heedlessness to the more fundamental malaise of human society. James Baldwin's bitter words to his nephew about remembering that to be born black was to be born 'a worthless human being' in a world of white supremacy must be heard and never cease to be heard, just as in a class-structured society the assumptions that govern relations must be brought into view. The social, economic and cultural distinctions of society throughout the world are so weighted with advantages and deprivations that praying itself can all too easily overlook them. A good deal of spirituality starts a long way beyond where the mass of mankind has been condemned to live, and 'we who pray' may forget to what an extent we are the assumptions we never question.

Now the christian faith is about men being loved by God, and christian prayer is the effort we make to observe that love. The Hebrew rumination upon this theme out of which Christ spoke and to which He gave flesh, had in the course of many centuries distinguished some fundamental features. It started from a community-in-the-making and insisted that the primary duty of life was to acknowledge God. Prayer enters the political world in that acknowledgement. It points to this pole of reference in all that is said and done in the people's life. What it understands of such an orientation of its life is expressed not in speculation about the nature of God but in the way that this people live under moral obligation. In every detail of their dealings with each other, in family life, trade, farming and personal relations, they are to act with justice, mercy, generosity and truth. They are likewise to deal with the stranger in such terms. Their culture is not at any time to be divorced from the worship of God. Political responsibility is thus sharply defined. George Steiner has quite recently described it as 'the blackmail of transcendence', the requirement that the human psyche and the culture of mankind shall not be self-contained but always open to the claim of God to the question of what He requires of both. Such people are to learn to be a holy people because the Lord your God is Holy. The truth and dignity of human life lie in the obligation to be answerable to Him, to learn to love Him in patient working out in everyday affairs of what love that knows no limit will require.

Such spirituality as this leaves nothing in the political or social or religious world unquestioned. It hammers away at all of them with certain simple tests: is this good enough for the sons of God? Is this what mercy and truth require? In a world situation where no questions are simple it insists upon certain priorities. The poor, the fatherless, the widows and the strangers, the weak who have no claim except their weakness, are made the test of true devotion. The Hebrew prophets made it clear that fasts and feasts had no validity as worship if they concealed a negligence towards the least of these. The stranger whose estrangement was his only title to be noticed was witness to the spiritual task to be performed. The oppressed may look repulsive, may be violent and brutal, may constitute a threat to the superior culture of the more 'advanced' society, a sub-humanity from which those human would protect themselves, but 'who taught the dog the trick they hanged him for?' and whose responsibility is put in question?

This sharp particularity of obligation towards the poor and the rejected gained its universal face in Jesus Christ, in His insistence that the keeping of the Law itself was but a disciplined awaiting of the act of God that alone gave significance and truth to human history. That act He called the coming of God's kingdom. He spoke of it as coming and already come. He charged men to be watchful and expectant of it. He taught them in their prayers to look for it. No other word could have made more intimate the engagement of God with men's affairs than this or turned politics – matters of public concern – into controversies between the Lord and His people. It affirmed the world and human history, saying Yes to them in no uncertain terms but looking for a responsive Yes from men and nations, a Yes that was consonant with the nature and will of Him who formed it. 'Thy Kingdom come' was to be a cry of joy, a marvelling exaltation of the heart of man that God should make the earth so glorious by His presence in it. It was likewise a warning note of all things put to judgement. Christ spoke of it in parables of growth, of search, of abrupt disclosure, of testing and of reckoning to be made. The Kingdom signified a life to be laid hold of here and now within the kingdoms of the world, a leaven at work to change the hearts and minds of men, a new perspective given to human history, a consummation of God's grand design. In common life on common earth, not in some ideal world of dreams or after-life, the people of God must look for the coming of His Kingdom. It was given to His friends and followers to announce its coming to the world, to work out in detail how to live as subjects of the Kingdom, to prove the freedom of a citizenship that made that of Rome look poor. They were to teach men so to pray that they might find some intimations of its glory in the conflict that embraced them, that like Stephen they might see the promise of its victory. Speech, silence, work, meals, marriage, parenthood, all were vehicles of the manifestation of its transfiguring power. A new mankind was coming to birth and the earth was once again the birthplace of the Man. 'Of Zion it shall be reported that he was born in her.'

Spirituality today must ask what has happened to this great vision of the Kingdom, with this Gospel engagement with the world of men. If this be truly the stuff and substance of our faith in Christ, why has our prayer become so little informed by it, so meagre in its hope, so timid and unexpectant? Why aren't we jubilant about the Kingdom's coming and passionate about its presence? Our self-examination must dig deep. To say Yes, not in the imagery of bygone days but in the politics and social matters of today, throws on to the communities of christians the twofold task of shaping the inner relationships of their own societies to embody their vision of the Kingdom and of witnessing in the entire world to the claims and marks of that Kingdom's coming. They must be asking hard searching questions about their own engagement with the world as it is, about the price they are paying for being tolerated or esteemed, about their silences and consents, about their own willingness to take trouble to ascertain the truth on any matter, about the style or standard of life they take for granted for some and not for others. They must be celebrating emancipation as a present condition of life by acting freely and bravely in public witness. They must see what the crisis of each decade is and re-order their life to face it. It is no bad test of spiritual awareness to ask in what ways is our mode of discipleship different from what it was ten or five years ago?

This is no easy time-serving but a sober and alert concern for the particularities of history now in the making. The most significant feature of this age is its experience of accelerative change and the technology which both assists it and enables men to deal with it. Men have now learned to make new tools so quickly and with such capacity that tools themselves begin to determine their lives. Such tools of complex character, as Ivan Illich shows, comprise our educational systems, their schools and colleges, manufacturing corporations and their handling of raw materials into consumer goods, health and security provision, transport and advertising media, finance and planning of public works. Men now living have already seen several epochs of such provision of tools, and the spectre that haunts their world is that of tools insisting on full employment and still greater elaboration. The alienation that Marx wrote of in the 1840s has taken on new proportions so that 'the world we have lost' is not simply a bygone age but a manner of living that has been eroded or overthrown.

Any Yes to God made with integrity of purpose must begin with a look at the Church and the churches as they have dealt with this task of awaiting the Kingdom. Two features of past history need to be examined because of their bearing on what we do now. Of the first we may say that it consists of the relations between the Church and the political powers of the time, the outcome of which is written deep in the social history of the world. The second concerns the intellectual and social changes that occurred, to which the Church so often responded with awkward and fearful reluctance. The two features were closely interwoven since it was the kind of choice made of relations with the political powers of the world that went far to determine the attitude of the Church to change of any kind. To disengage and re-engage ourselves we have to consider what was done.

Dialogue with the world is now widely spoken of as being the pressing business of the Church. It presupposes detachment on the one hand and a deep sense of involvement on the other, together with a freedom to speak of a quite radical nature. It will not be done in any depth apart from a close scrutiny of what took place in earlier times. There are and have been throughout history a number of sects that stood apart and endeavoured to live as colonies of heaven. The churches made arrangements of a different kind and drew upon the Scriptures for their justification. The Bible was, in Walter Ullmann's words, 'a ready-made philosophy relative to matters of public government', and from it could be drawn such teaching, rightly or wrongly, as that men were subjects of the princely powers and owed a strict obedience to them. It was a far cry from the common ground of dialogue. Resistance to superior authority was out of the question. What rights men had were purely a concession to them by majesty itself. The public weal depended on outright suppression of all opinion contrary to the assumptions of divinely given authority. Prayer for all kings and those set in authority expressed assurance of such an ordering of human life, and scarcely contemplated change. That somewhere down the social scale a different way of thinking of the law and of the rights of men appeared, that change however slight must sometime put in question this fixed scheme of things, was felt with some unease. In the later Middle Ages new notions of citizenship began to gain attention in men's minds. The seed-bed of a new conception of society and human rights was being sown. The changes were interwoven with the widespread growth of popular devotion and recourse to prayer which flourished at some distance from the great centres of hierarchical control. The churches, catholic and reformed, maintained as firmly as they could the older notions of authority and obedience. Erasmus and his friends, though keenly critical of them could find no way of altering them. To Luther no such need appealed. The effects of such authoritative systems continued to influence the churches until today.

The price paid for such a scheme of things was heavy, and payment is still in arrears. As political structures in Europe hardened in the seventeenth century and open conflicts like the English civil war broke out, as the churches compromised themselves still further in support of authoritarian régimes, there set in that terrible divorce between the institutional life of the churches and the political, intellectual and social movements which were to refashion the life of European man and to change the outlook of the world. It meant that the Yes to life which issued from those who sought release from oppression, illiteracy, squalor, disease, injustice and poverty was made in defiance of the known attitude of the authorities in the churches. Despite the heroic efforts of turbulent priests to champion the oppressed, despite the charity and tenderness that sounded a new note in the teaching on prayer of François de Sales, it was commonly believed by those who suffered most that the Church was 'on the other side'. It is the case today that many sincere and honest christians have no conception of the extent to which the spirituality of the christian church is written off by those in every nation who care most for social justice and the fashioning of humaner life for all mankind. The Yes to God that is needed most is that which most humbly acknowledges first of all a pride, a lust for power, a cynicism, an insensitiveness to human suffering which went far to alienate the oppressed of the earth from the Church of Jesus Christ, and which, we may believe, made much of its spirituality stink in the nostrils of the Lord God of all the earth. Without such penitence, it may be said, the Yes to God stands in danger of being foolishly complacent.

The situation was made worse by the failure of the Church to teach men to pray faithfully and hopefully in the face of the great revolutions, political, economic and scientific, which broke up the old patterns of their life. What was missing was an understanding of the significance of these conflicts for the souls of men. The Church had been for too long absorbed in its own narrowly ecclesiastical conception of the social order, too concerned for its own institutional safety, to be generously disposed to its critics. Because men were afraid their sensibilities were warped and dulled. In the debates upon the question of the American colonies, Burke had magnificently declared that 'magnanimity in politics is not seldom the truest wisdom, and a great empire and little minds go ill together', but magnanimity in prayer, so much more sorely needed, was not a characteristic feature of the times. It was not that the condition of the poor was entirely forgotten; it was noted and commended to them as the excellent device of providence to teach them habits of frugality and thrift. It was not that new houses of prayer were not being built in the great new centres of the working population with a just proportion of free seats to encourage the attendence of the poor, but they were not designed to nurture a spirituality whose radical Yes might be an axe laid to the roots of trees of social complacency. While movements of reform and social amelioration got under way, the churches, for the most part, stood aside, not understanding, not seeking to understand, the new world being fashioned.

A spirituality for today which does not begin by looking as closely and clearsightedly as possible at this background lacks that needed particularity of engagement and that acquaintance with the marks of the Passion without which a Yes to God of any reality cannot be made. Prayer seeks to grasp the truth, in this case the truth of social life, and as long as social fantasies possess the minds and hearts of men, the truth stands little chance of gaining their attention. Prayer is paying attention, taking all the trouble in the world to pay attention, to the condition of the other person and other persons without limit. It means, no less, paying attention to the assumptions of our own lives, of our position in society, of the social class we belong to, and whose standards of life we would otherwise scarcely notice. It has been the manifest failure of christians in the past to take seriously the question of class, to appreciate class-consciousness, to note the consequences of class distinctions, which has gone far to render their spirituality poor and mean. What God affirms, men cannot afford to neglect.

Prayer is not just thinking about these social problems, but seeing them as the concern of God and therefore as the concern of those who claim to love Him and want to serve Him. It sends those who pray to think and work out what needs to be done, and it brings them back to pray still more over what has thus been done to Him, to look once again at the Yes we have dared to say. True praying endeavours to look more closely into the nature of that Yes. Like the man seeking goodly pearls it must be for ever ready to give what it has for the sake of the truer Yes. We can look back from today and see how, for example, the efforts of men like Kingsley and Maurice were so maimed by their class-assumptions, their paternalism, their distrust of the working men, and their own idealised version of the christian faith, that their work though genuine in intention was as far from the reality of the problems of industrialised England as the novels of Charlotte Yonge. The warning is made to us today. There is in the final volume of Charles Booth's *Life and Labour of the People of London*, published in 1903, a comment upon the outcome of the whole work. 'We see life cursed by drink, brutality and vice, and loaded down by ignorance and poverty, religion paralysed by its own inconsistencies, and administration wrapped in the swaddling clothes of indecision and mutual distrust.' The details of that scene have changed, but praying must needs be asking to see whether something more fundamental remains untouched, unattempted, unmarked. Booth saw the void between man and man, and he drew in rough outlines the picture that sociological studies today have carried much further throughout the world, but the spiritual issues that these have laid bare have hardly begun to transform our lines of approach. The brief expedition of the French worker-priests, the scattered guerrilla work of communes and lives hidden deep in the cities and shantytowns, the passionate identification of some men and women with the despised and the rejected, point the way forward to a path 'we' must make our own.

It is time to say final words about this 'we' whose intention is to try to say Yes to God in this world which so heavily engages men and women in conditions that threaten to silence that word.

We are first of all required to be watchful, our first prayer – 'Lord that I may receive my sight.' If we mean this, we shall see both marvellous things of His glory and terrible things of His agony. Do 'we' want to go on with this?

Secondly, we shall see our calling. It is addressed to all men, it is personal and therefore for everyman. It is a summons to get up from where we are and go forward seeking a different standard of life. There are no blue-prints of what it is like, no schedules of its location. A certain foolishness attaches itself to the undertaking, for it cannot claim to see its objective or destination. It is very open to mockery, and 'we' may be more often than not among those who have lost their way.

Thirdly, 'we' are those who expect enormously. We expect to be met in quite unforeseeable ways and times by the Christ of faith, to discover Him present 'as He will be present', in the terms and manner He chooses to come in. In picturesque terms we may say that He set out to look for us long since, long before it occurred to us to look for Him, but we none the less expect to be found. The end of it all was prefigured in Christ whose Passion was pledge to the world that He would stay in it and be found there and known for Who He is.

Fourthly, we expect, though we set out alone and are often alone, to be joined by others, by the oddest company that imagination could conceive of ('motley's your only wear'), for this is not a private venture but a common shared undertaking of the people of God.

Fifthly, we put ourselves into this with the oddest of all human hopes, of forgetting who we were and discovering who we are, of finding ourselves addressed by a new name and answering to it because we know that it is our own.

6 Spirituality and Sexual Love

'What is disquieting about the time is not so much its open and avowed materialism but what it takes to be its spirituality.'
Irving Babbitt, *Democracy and Leadership*.

'The present "crisis of the couple" is only one aspect of the crisis of the sacred.'
Suzanne Lilar, *Aspects of Love*.

NEED WE SPEAK OF SEX IN A BOOK ON PRAYING? DOES our attempt to say Yes to God involve bringing this aspect of life, not simply into captivity to Christ, but into the Gracehoper's joyicity as that which we most long to do? What indeed do we mean by calling it an aspect of life, and how far dare we say that spirituality in the Western world has dealt wisely and lovingly with sexuality and sexual relations? At the very threshold of christian devotion stands the figure of a woman, a woman both humiliated and exalted, though not yet clothed with the sun, a woman whose Yes to God was the simplest and most profound affirmation of willing acceptance of God's engagement with mankind. Without doubt, the Blessed Virgin has been hailed throughout the centuries by men and women with love and trust, and at times accorded a queenly dignity. But on the threshold men are busy with their own affairs, hurrying on to give their minds to plans and purposes of their own, and she, herself a temple of God's making, with her own significant and secret rites, has stood unmarked in her great representative capacity. It may be more important than anything else in human life today that men and women should pause upon the threshold of the house of life again, and stand together there and ponder on this 'and' that joins them, and learn to say a Yes together such as human history has not yet heard.

Three things may be noted first. Here, in our day to day lives, engagement and passion are deeply involved. In common usage passion and passionate mean little else than erotic desire. Engagement announces a projected marriage. With sexuality we face a great hunger, a great drive of human energy, a perception of beauty, an enrichment of human variety, a late biological development, an intense pleasure, that challenges those divided by it to seek and find at another level a unity of being. It is also to be seen as a gift from God, which means it is charged with a character described as holy, an awesome and often explosive thing. Misused it can blast and wither and empty of all significance the human beings foolish enough to mistake it, baulked and perverted it can poison relationships between human beings and between humanity and God. Gifts of such dangerous potentiality can neither be ignored nor handed back. The primitive impulse to deify sexual love was not wholly misguided; it has all the features of great mystical experience, abandon, ecstasy, polarity, dying, rebirth and perfect union. It continues as the most popular of ancient idolatries in our midst, and has in our own day acquired new prophets to expound its most solemn mysteries. It prompts between human beings those features characteristic of prayer; a noticing, a paying attention, a form of address, a yearning to communicate at ever deeper levels of being, an attempt to reach a certain communion with the other. It holds out suggestion of personal fulfilment, of union achieved, of community known. Love poetry, whether of the *Song of Songs* or of the epithalamium of today, pre-empts the language of devotion as of right. The austere purity of the Phoenix and the Turtle is Love's Athanasian Creed:

> *Reason, in itself confounded,*
> *Saw division grow together,*
> *To themselves yet either neither,*
> *Simple were so well compounded.*

> *That it cried, How true a twain*
> *Seemeth this concordant one.*
> *Love hath reason, reason none,*
> *If what parts, can so remain.*

All of which prompts the question how it may be that men and women should live through the fullest experiencing of their sexuality as their road to God, or whether the roads divide, and as so often in the past the highest spiritual life is construed as meaning the renunciation of sexuality.

In the second place, we cannot be happy about either past or current experience of sexual relationships. We need not wholly accept Dr Alex Comfort's contention that Christianity has dealt more savagely with sexuality than other religions, but we must hear out the charges made and admit that its handling of it has been far from satisfactory, far too faithless about love and forgiveness, far too little critical of social custom, far too heavily influenced by a celibate clergy, far too fearful and cruelly unimaginative. This was not the best ground from which to say Yes to God. When Coleridge described the praying of his day as 'tongue-tied' and contrasted it with the exuberance that was shown by Jeremy Taylor and much more so by St Teresa, he ascribed its poverty to the influence of fears that one might be saying the wrong things, giving oneself away, mixing up things that shouldn't be there. He was commenting upon the condition of mind that as regards sexuality had been for many generations of Christians tongue-tied with misgivings if not branded with horror. Examples are obvious. The failure to speak confidently about sexual desire, the exaltation of virginity at the expense of the coupled life, the terrible inadequacy of teaching about both marriage and parenthood, left the great mass of human beings bereft of the help they most truly needed. The greatest features of their lives, for good or ill, were being set aside. The failure was most conspicuous and most revealing in its treatment of the status of women. The ambiguous Pauline legacy, however handled in catholic or in protestant traditions, could do little to help and much to hinder in the shaping of an encouraging sexual ethic and a spirituality that divinised the coupled life. Had the claims of the Church to possession of truth been less arrogant less harm might well have been done. The foreground of human existence was never quite freed from the evil-smelling pronouncements of some of the great Fathers of the Church, and the consequences were impoverishing, divisive, prurient and frustrating. The too-ready acquiescence of the christian Church in the political, economic and cultural institutions of the Roman Empire and its successor states went far to negate the possibilities of new freedom in love and of genuine community which the Gospel proclaimed, and substituted an idealised version of the new life for a simple and faithful attempt to live out its promise in Christ. That some couples found their way to become heirs together of the grace of life must be beyond doubt. There were those like Elizabeth of Hungary and her Ludwig, whose pure passion broke through the restrictive walls and kindled a fearless natural burning love, not to be called either sacred or profane, but seen as the incandescence of body and soul. What was missing was a joyous glad-hearted recognition of the transforming power of love in the coupled life, of the ministries of both men and women towards each other and through each other to God. To have muted the Yes in this field of life was a grievous thing.

We come now to the present scene. That something akin to a revolution in awareness of sexuality is in process of expansion is clear enough both in thought and practice. Since Freud, its implications have been so widened as to embrace all aspects of human life. There have not been wanting those teachers who have proclaimed it to be the very key to human affairs, who have taught salvation by sex. The loosening of the social structures inherited from the past under the impact of wars and revolutions, of science and technology, weakened their sanctions of social direction and enabled a number of counter-cultures to flourish and proselytise, not without effect upon the thinking and teaching of the Church itself. The most striking change has come with the dispersal of the cloud of secrecy, with the beginnings of attempts to find adequate language for the honest and serious conversation that sex invites and requires. The presentation of the nature of sexuality in the novel and drama and on television screens has become so detailed and explicit, even if still inadequate, that the rough categorising of the sexes and the aspects of love that obtained in the past are challenged by claims for more sensitive discernment and discrimination. The great novelists of the nineteenth century could be accused, as Kathleen Nott has said, of failing to tell the truth about either the pleasures or problems of sexual love. Their successors may be failing still but not for want of attempts to do so. It is probable that since the days of *Pamela* until now the novel has been one of the most influential factors in the forming of popular thought about sex. *Lady Chatterley's Lover* may well have been a poor confused book but it symbolised much of the movement towards a new freedom to speak of the experiences of sex. But honesty of purpose and seriousness of treatment must contend with a sea of sexual fantasy flooding across the affluent societies of the modern world, driven on by commercial exploitation but itself the witness to the pitiful lack of sexual fulfilment and happiness throughout that world. Boredom on the one hand and craving for excitement on the other tell their own dismal tale of failed sexual relations.

It is because prayer is concerned with elucidation that it must engage itself with this, must receive the intimations of passion with an unfrightened uncensorious confident effort to welcome this gift of God. The situation is not one to be resolved into a defensive battle for some standard of sexual behaviour approved by the few or the many, but an occasion for a great bid for more informed and imaginative understanding of conjugal love, of the social and psychological difficulties bearing upon it, of the factors at work to aid or attack it. There is a great balance of injustice, hatred, blindness and cruel insensitiveness to redress and make reparation for on behalf of women. There is equally great need to rescue men from a fearful legacy of self-hatred and tormented distrust of sexuality which has maimed and so often robbed them of their opportunities to grow through sexual relations to greater maturity of living. The burden is formidable. Podsnappery is as ingeniously bland as ever in blurring the real issues to be faced, and sexual jealousy a quick and easily kindled hateful power.

A Yes to God that springs from a joyful perception of sexual distinction and union, which sees it not as something needing to be sanctified by a sacrament but in itself as sacred and able to nourish a rich growing awareness of the sacred in human life, which can relate its ecstasies to the whole range of conjugal and domestic chores, bringing it down to earth not as a degradation and despoiling of its splendour but as a transforming action, can issue only from a greatly changed assimilation of its character in prayer. It must bespeak conviction on the part of christian people in a quite new way and a new humility in the face of such obvious failures in the past. There can be few tracts of human experience in which a confession of folly and pride is more immediately demanded. Yet there are many inclined to protest that the sexual theme already commands too much attention. They would wish, without denying its vast importance, to have reflection upon prayer lifted to that plane where there is neither male nor female. Behind their plea is a long tradition of what looks like a-sexual spirituality. They would point to many great classics of christian devotion and books on prayer-life from which specific sexual reference was quite clearly absent. They might ask us to say if we thought such works were any the worse for that. Does sexuality pertain to the personal life, to the life of the soul, to such an extent that praying must take such account of it? Two books may be briefly considered with this in mind.

Contemplative prayer is treated with great theological learning and a deep desire to help men and women to pray in a book entitled *On Prayer* by Hans Urs von Balthasar. It engages the reader from within the teaching and practice of the great Catholic heritage and uses its traditional proven resources to give a sound foundation to the efforts of those attempting to pray drawn from this long experience of the people of God. It contains so much that it seems almost perverse to notice omissions, but something important is lacking. It would be untrue to say that it contains no reference to matters of sex since fatherhood, motherhood, brides, bridegrooms and the union of two persons in one flesh, together with the 'raptures of love' and 'blissful intercourse' are mentioned. Yet it is clear that these are there as illustrative terms, or as examples drawn from life, to illuminate the spiritual intercourse of contemplation. The experiences and relationships to which they refer are important for the author's purpose in a figurative sense. This is legitimate enough but it does not carry us on to pondering upon the spiritual experience that comes from within marriage, parenthood, marital breakdown, loss of a partner and a great range of sexual problems. These things for the majority of people constitute life itself and they want to know how to pray them, or, since prayer and play are now so linked together, how to play them out in an affirmative way. How does the 'mystical union betwixt Christ and His Church' come to mean anything unless the most intimate union known to men and women is enabled to yield its own truths not as illustrations of something else but as their way to God? There is something finally unhelpful in shifting attention elsewhere. If there is one pervasive danger about all talk of spirituality it is that of putting asunder that which God has joined, separating the 'religious' features from the rest of human experience. In Mark Rutherford's novel *Catherine Furze* there is an illuminating comment upon this matter. It falls to a non-churchgoing doctor to speak about the marriage of the clergyman in the story. He has perceived the estrangement of this man and wife, he has reflected a good deal upon the desertion in spirit that it reveals, and he speaks with great deliberation. 'There is a bit of excellence stuck down before him for him to value. It is not intended for others, but for him, and he deserts the place appointed him by nature if he neglects it.' It is the use of the word 'neglect' which is most important because it is the failure to see and work away at the connection between the immediate relationships we have with each other and our relation with God that goes far to retard our growth as people of God, so that we come unprepared to face the great questions that God will put to us. Yes goes by default again and again because the occasions of learning how it is to be made have been lost in the sexual field. Somewhere without doubt the love of husband, wife and children is challenged by a still greater claim of God, somewhere beyond 'dull sublunary lovers' love' there is the supreme engagement of God with man, the 'Thou art mine' that is the fundamental disclosure of divine solicitude, but men do not come to the knowledge of this but by learning the first steps towards it in the experience of love, the bit of excellence, already afforded to them. So while von Balthasar insists that 'contemplation does not aim at remoteness from the earth', nor 'does it see earthly reality as a mere shadow, or maybe a screen shrouding the world of heaven', it is difficult to see where this earthly reality is seriously encountered. Conditions of work, war, sickness, politics, sex, racialism and deprivation do not enter into the discussion of how prayer is to be exercised. Yet these are the actual conditions in which the nature of love is perceived, in which men rise or fail to rise to its occasions. There is a timelessness which ignores the pressures of time and circumstance upon changing ageing human beings, so that the day to day dying which is so real a part of our life gets little attention.

A second illustration may be taken from the volume entitled *Spirituality Today*, a report of a conference held at Durham in 1967. Papers were read at this gathering upon such subjects as personal growth, psychology, living in the world, the future of man, together with theology and philosophy, but at no point were the problems raised by sexuality made the centre of attention. Not even words like adolescence and anxiety were led to consideration of the sexual factor. It was a paper on the contribution of monasticism to spirituality which alone thought fit to refer to 'the need for sexual happiness', and to admit that 'not every attempt to live with a woman is a success'. It was to be noted further that among seven or eight distinguished speakers room was found only for one woman. That this should be the case in a gathering designed to grapple with the great problems of contemporary life as they bear upon spirituality was an odd reflection of the way in which experience itself can be set aside. Love was invoked, but strangely enough though poets were quoted, no line from the great love-poems was ever recalled. Did no one yearn to interpret spirituality with the passion of Giuseppe Caponsacchi or to propound the problems of engagement in the complicated issues which beauty itself gives rise to?

> *But she . . .*
> *The glory of life, the beauty of the world,*
> *The splendour of heaven . . . well, sirs, does no one move?*
> *Do I speak ambiguously? The glory, I say,*
> *And the beauty, I say, and the splendour, still say I,*
> *Who, a priest, trained to live my whole life long*
> *On beauty and splendour, solely at their source*
> *God, have thus recognised my food in one . . .*

It is the fact that we are not sufficiently moved by the beauty and the splendour as it comes to us in the course of everyday life in sexual union, 'a thing men seldom miss', and have not been sufficiently ready to utilise what reflection upon it by poets and artists can give that has made so much of our spirituality something less personal than it should have been. Too much of human life, including prayer, remains arrested at an adolescent stage.

To say that there is an urgency in this matter is not a concession to various belligerent counter-cultures or liberationist movements, but to take more serious notice of the impact upon the lives of men and women of the breakdown of traditional codes of behaviour, and the lack of confident relating of the masculine and feminine features of human life in the society of today. We live in an age which talks and sings endlessly of love but does little to rescue it from its largely idealised and fictional conceptions which it inherited from the traditions of courtly love. Possessed of vast means of glamorising the romantic aspects of the erotic, Western society has as yet done little to bring eros and agape together in a pattern of conjugal love, and the christian Church, in spite of its incarnational theology and its knowledge of 'our lovely human nature' has not greatly helped human beings to fashion a positive approach to the redemption of eros. There has been all too little partnership in facing the difficulties of sexual relations, of inequalities, of exploitation, of open antagonism, too great a readiness to put all the emphasis upon stable marriages and good housekeeping without inquiring too deeply whether other aspects of the sexual relationship were not wretchedly abused or ignored. Such a spirituality tended to avoid the profound questions that tension raised and failed to make the part to be played by the woman a clear and vivid example of the way in which partners to an engagement continually transform their relations with each other.

> *O, I must feel your brain prompt mine,*
> *Your heart anticipate my heart,*
> *You must be just before, in fine,*
> *See, and make me see, for your part,*
> *New depths in the divine.*

Failing in this, it could scarcely begin to contemplate spirituality playing a more decisive part in the human Yes to God.

Yet the change has come in this, as in other features of modern life, the break has been made, and it rests with christians to take up the challenge offered to them. They could have no better introduction to the matter than the reflections made by Henry Adams in his book *Mont St. Michel and Chartres* upon the power of the twelfth-century devotion to the Blessed Virgin and his relating of this to the power of the dynamo as he brooded over the Great Exposition of 1900. Adams offered no explanation of that astonishing outpouring of energy that built some eighty cathedrals and hundreds of vast churches, kindled a great enterprise of human reason, inspired a new wave of lyrical delight, which devotion to the Virgin set going. In sheer expenditure of human resources, it has been said, there is no parallel outside the efforts of modern warfare in European history. At the heart of it as the focus of its initiative and devotion was the Mother with her Son, the Queen of Heaven. It was the conviction of her presence, of her personal delight in being there among her people, of her tastes to be consulted and met with pleasure, of her gracious approval of what was done in honour of her queenly dignity, that gave to every feature in it the sense of not only being surprised by but swept along by joy. It was an engagement that gripped the imagination as never before. Whether we pause to look at the grave figures of the porches at Chartres or stare up at the cattle hoisted to the heavens at Laon or marvel at the upsoaring of the vault at Beauvais, it is to the figure of the woman in whom the inspiration took life that we must needs return. From her men drew the strength, delight, beauty and sense of wonder that issued in a rapturous Yes. The woman, mused Adams, had once been such a force among mankind, but what of the future? What artist or poet dared insist on the power of sex in the modern world? More important still, what conception of woman in relation to man could spark off another and more profound engagement of the spirit in man? While Adams wrote, the beginnings of the change which has assumed the character of a revolution were already apparent. What is still in doubt is the nature of the Yes to God that such changes call for. Passion without engagement, we said earlier, ran recklessly to waste, but passion engaged with fantasy such as has inspired the generation of *Playboy* could have no consequence but a desolation of spirit and a widening of the estrangement between men and women. Something more fundamental than the ordination of women, however desirable that may be, is at question in the issues raised for modern spirituality by the sexual upheaval today. We are at a point where prayer itself must search unweariedly for a new and authentic Yes, where men and women together must speak to each other with an honesty and openness for which there are no precedents to appeal to. We underestimate the gravity of our predicament as human beings if we suppose that the relationship of the sexes need not be a profoundly important matter for spirituality today.

It has been said with great force by Harvey Cox that because the Gospel has ceased to be for many young adults today an occasion of a liberating Yes being made and an induction into personhood and genuine community, the Gospel must be demythologised and delegalised to enable it to be a means of new engagement. But this is very largely a diversion of attention to resources and means rather than confrontation with the real problem. In the concluding words of *Civilisation and its Discontents*, Freud raised the fateful question of the ability of mankind to master the self-destructiveness now poised for human extermination, and expressed an expectation that the eternal eros would put forth his strength to meet the challenge. Is Saul also among the prophets? What he sought was an outpouring of the spirit of love able to surmount the contraries and contradictions experienced by man and to bind together in one community of fellowship the diverse elements of humanity, an energy capable of achieving such unification. Where the twelfth century in Europe had drawn from its devotion to the Blessed Virgin its great exuberance of creativity, it fell to the men and women of today to discover for themselves a like energising principle, an impulse of spirituality commensurate with the needs of the time. It had to be, like its forerunners, grounded deep in the earth, in the consciousness of men and women, and it had to soar towards the heavens in a growing unity of purpose, a consciousness of community, of mankind unified, divinised and expectant of the Christ. Such indeed is Teilhard de Chardin's vision, and it is noteworthy that he himself turned to consider where the needed activation of mankind to engage itself with such a task could lie and saw its locus in sexuality, in the love that poured forth from its polarity. But it was a sexuality in action at a new level of human engagement that was called for, a new kind of Yes to God in which every ordinary man and woman would participate in learning to love each other as never before. The youngsters were not wrong in shouting 'Make Love not War', but what was to be learned was what making love involved. The sexuality of the past had to a large extent set marriage and family life and reproduction apart from and even in opposition to the matter of loving. What was now needed to give man heart to press on with his tremendous task was just such inspiration as the cathedral builders had drawn from the cult of the Virgin. They must find it now in a new relationship between the sexes. 'Not in flight from (by suppressing them) but in mastery of (by sublimating them) the unfathomable spiritual forces that still lie dormant beneath the mutual attraction of the sexes – there lie the hidden essence of chastity and the grand task it will have to face.' Teilhard had gone boldly to the springs of love, never doubting that however befouled or misused they had been in the past they could run clean again, could run with such copious power as was yet undreamt of, could re-energise mankind to undertake its critical task. The coupled life, disciplined by a new perception of chastity, renewed by new awareness of sexual cohesion, took on a wholly changed significance. The Miltonic vision gained new splendour.

> *The world was all before them, where to choose*
> *Their place of rest, and Providence their guide.*
> *They, hand in hand, with wandering steps and slow,*
> *Through Eden took their solitary way.*

The task of spirituality then in this field lies in such engagement with the art of loving, in the removal of the burdens of exploitation and inequality, of fear and of authority, in patient attention to the wounds and pain of body and spirit that the two sexes have inflicted upon each other in the past. We cannot say Yes to God in the depth required of us today unless men and women can say yes to each other in the fullness of their sexuality. The antagonisms and deep differences have to be faced. All that is concentrated in Desdemona's sight, 'O, these men, these men', or in Namier's words, 'I've loved disastrously little', is nevertheless to be taken as part of the pain of the engagement that promises to yield a still greater Yes.

If praying is to do its full part in this it must likewise be grounded in an honest avowal and conviction of the goodness of sexuality notwithstanding all the confusions and problems it brings. Half a century ago, in an address on the 'Facts and truths concerning the soul which are of the utmost importance in the life of prayer', von Hügel named among seven such facts 'a right attitude towards the sex-instinct, and, as to what is, for the christian, the sin of sins'. It sounds ominously familiar – sex under the heading of sin, if not as the sin of sins, and irregular sexual relations as 'living in sin'. But von Hügel was saying no such things. He was rather trying in his solid painstaking way to say the very opposite. With all the caution that was characteristic of his writing, he nevertheless insisted upon a positive acceptance of sexuality, and said clearly that 'not even St Augustine dared censure the sex-instinct as such'. Here it was, a God-given power entrusted to weak human creatures, its creativity coupled with and exposed to quite perilous possibilities of vicious defilement, its rapturous abandonment, ecstasy and self-giving threatening always to break loose from nurturing relationships, itself both earnest of and hungry for that joyicity that the Gracehoper must seek in God. What the right attitude to it must be, von Hügel anchored firmly in a sense of awed, glad and painstaking use of the singular gifts of God, which can sound pedestrian enough in speaking of passionate desire but which carried with it a profound conviction of the way in which God must be honoured in man's body. It was about as far from Benjamin Franklin's 'use of venery' as it could be. 'No grace,' says von Hügel abruptly, 'without the substrata, the occasion, the material of nature', and if, as any man knows, the substrata are still fiery and volcanic and eruptive, blasting great rents in the terrain of everyday life, this too must be taken as part of our holding to God. Did we not speak of Him in terms of fire? Must we not run the risk of being scorched?

And the sin of sins? Here von Hügel is explicit and brief; not lust but pride and self-sufficiency.

Western spirituality has jumped and struggled like a frightened horse at such a situation. The difficulties have been experienced in all the traditions in which men and women have prayed. It has been said that in spite of the plentiful use of erotic imagery in Hasidic spirituality, for example, 'women are not normally within the full scope of the Hasidic doctrines on prayer', and this points to a widespread failure to admit in practice, to do more than idealise, the full necessary engagement of the two sexes in any satisfactory Yes to God. For christians it has been a continuing test of the reality of their faith in the hallowing of all things, of their conviction that love, human and divine, presents one face not two. 'Love cannot be "purely human" for its genesis lies elsewhere', and when Jewish Franz Rosenzweig spoke of the *Song of Songs* as the focal book of revelation, he meant to assert that indissoluble union. It has been the sad burden of men to forget this and the hard lot of women to endure it being doubted; hardest of all to find it degraded or turned to a fiction, deprived of its roots in the obvious God-given earth of conjugal union. Herein has lain, however little understood, the Passion wrought in the inmost being of mankind. Investing His love in the flesh and blood of His creatures, in its sexual drives and erotic delights as in its patient endurance and cherishing of beauty, God took the risk that it would be defiled and maimed, mocked and exploited. He did not reserve this gift of Himself in love till men had grown wise or tender-hearted enough to value and use it well. He uttered His Yes in the flesh and waited for man's response. Our Yes in sexuality has been long delayed, and even now is pronounced in hesitant fashion. In his book *God is a New Language* Dom Sebastian Moore has asked us to see 'the measure of our lostness', the failure of our vision of the divine, in the writing on the wall, in the scribbed graffiti of the public lavatory; to see it as the pathetic evidence of men's inability or unwillingness to see what God had chosen to reveal to them, of their choosing rather to mock themselves in their begetting and their consummation, of their stopping their own ears to the life-giving word. It is a measure of lostness because it cries out like the goddams of St Joan in rejection of love that comes to it, because like the Beast of the childhood story it longs for release by Beauty.

It is not only in crude obscenity that love is lost to sight. The rabbis might say with genuine gladness that the Shekinah dwelt between a husband and a wife, but this also might be the very place where unschooled by grace and staled by custom men's eyes might be holden that they should not perceive that glory. All too often we blunder into the sanctuaries and holy places and ignore the signals of transcendence. To treat love, as in Byron's much quoted line, as something apart from the real life of a man is to reject the terms of the engagement offered by God in maturing deepening sexual relationship, and to thrust men themselves towards that condition described by Lawrence as 'crucified by sex'. The description is no hyperbole, for sexuality, as men and women in moments of truth well know, is not something that they themselves dispose, but carries its own intention and that not a purely biological one but something much more inclusive that may fairly be called the creative will of God at work in mankind. Conjugal union represents that creative-redemptive act in our midst. It is most intimately personal and inclusive of all life. It can be reduced to a mere mockery of this as much by selfish self-centred marital egoism as by a profligate squandering of its treasures. In spite of his Don Juan affectations down the ages, man has known this throughout; sex has retained a problematic character, a sense of shame has haunted the manifest inability of the conscious will to exercise complete control of a man's mind and body, a yearning for completion in the woman and that beyond-herself which she represents has never ceased to inspire men to attempt in fear and trembling that which bespeaks not conquest nor possession but union itself. No writer has more vehemently, more tragically and more finely expressed this than Tolstoy, both in living and writing, whether in profligacy and rage against the woman who invites man to it, or in purged gladness at the sight of an Eden-like springtime in union with her. What spirituality today is most clearly summoned to attempt among men and women together is a greater venture of faith made towards the relationship of communion in which both may learn new meanings of engagement and passion.

In the novel *Chance*, Conrad speaks many times of the passive aspect of womanly existence. He takes care each time he does so to make clear that he does not mean lack of animation, energy, courage and wisdom on her part. He is concerned to describe her endurance, her capacity to wait, to bear cruelty and rejection, to remain sensitive and hopeful, to be forgiving, realistic and merciful. He means by it too a power to sensitise men to a new perception, however briefly retained, of the meaning of love itself. It is the novelist's picture of something held up to the world in the Passion of Christ, the passionate passiveness of which in its closing temporal stages the women were left in contemplation. In the vision of conjugal union towards which our spirituality must point today, it is this feminine understanding of love and the energy it commands which must become its inspiring factor. Significantly enough, in the great outpouring of human energy in the twelfth century in which the idealised figure of the woman played so large a part, the stirrings of an understanding of love of this feminine kind became part of the consciousness of European culture. No doubt great numbers of women had suffered in silence but endured in love before Héloïse wrote her letters to Abélard which now remain to witness to what appears to be the utter defeat of love. Humanly speaking, she lost everything but what she expressed was a rapturous faith in a conjugal love whose lineaments our modern world even now endeavours to trace out. Héloïse took it as far as she could, it is still spoken of as a memorial to her, and if she found no man and no Church ready to sustain her, so that she was compelled to bear her passion alone, her defeat remains an indissoluble part of love's victory for ever.

We are looking at the revelation of love, to be honoured in its erotic as in all its characteristic features, sublimated by its reference to God from whom it takes its origin, subjected to such regulative chastity as a maturing wonder at its nature would rejoice in, and recognising that it will be perceived only by those who stay awake to watch for it. It comes as the old doctor in William de Morgan's novel *Joseph Vance* says, like a shaft of sunlight on the walls of a tunnel through which we are passing, and it speaks of the true light from which in our faithlessness we so often turn away. But it does not go away; it promises rather at each showing of itself to come again. To pray is to wait for its coming. All its manifestations in their infinite diversity are but foretastes of the splendour to be revealed. Héloïse's monument is not her own letters but Peter of Cluny's letter to her when Abélard was dead, itself a perfect witness to an awareness of the presence of love in life. A Yes is being uttered by stammering lips but it grows in grace and strength. When we look at the slow but deliberate movement of the *béguines* in the Low Countries from the twelfth century onwards, we find women braving the hostility and the contempt of men, pressing forward with a quietly confident transfiguring grasp of the erotic element in human make-up and perceiving what nuptial union prefigures in the communication of the soul with God. The Yes to God takes flesh with dreadful suffering but 'it moves', survives the hatred and the fear which would reject it, and carries its note of hope to all successive generations. It is rooted in that which is common to all, in the life of each person whose earliest knowledge of love comes simply from being touched and held and fed by another, whose growth to person-hood comes through that baffling and painful distinction from the other, whose hope of true life comes with the experience of being drawn to love the other, to make of it a glad and trustful Yes.

We stand in need then of a spirituality which, in this present fermentation of sexuality, addresses itself quite humbly to learn the truth of nuptial union as never before. For too long men have been buying and selling and pitifully bargaining in the outer court of the Temple. It is not to be wondered at if few were able to make their way further into the house of God – which temple you are – unspoiled and uncontaminated by all the huckstering that has gone on. All of us have been damaged by it. Here and there we have paused to listen to those who spoke of the pure beauty of this unity in love, of this miracle and mystery we sought, but though the precious thing was put into our hands we impatiently and foolishly let it fall and turned to listen to the hucksterers again. We could not believe that such love could be freely given or that it came not as a finished thing but as the proved attainment of a lifetime's labour of love. But now we have to learn how en-gagement and passion must take our flesh and bring us to the experience of a fusion, a making one, so complete that the 'we' being thus formed would be to both the partners the reality of their lives. It is said that women have always believed in this. It is certain that it is their part in life to show the meaning of it to men, to be themselves the bearers of the continuing revelation of love, just as one woman once bore the revelation of the love di-vine. Men will continue, for this is their part, to build a temple dedicated to it. Women so honoured and invited into it will be, as through the ages they have been, not a little puzzled and fright-ened by what they have found there, but as they have tried in faith to make it a dwelling to live in, clean and furnished for the dwellers and the guest they expect, so now when a new venture of faith is called for, will be more than ever engaged in their God-given task. Together the two sexes are to build and furnish the house in which it pleaseth Him to dwell.

7 Prayer and the Personal

'The one thing that matters is that we always say Yes to God whenever we experience Him.'

Julian of Norwich, *Revelations of the Divine Love.*

'and yes I said yes I will yes.'

James Joyce, *Ulysses.*

THERE WAS A WONDERFUL DICKENS' BABY WHOSE TEETHing troubles prevented her from 'being herself', but as the expected tooth did not come through, 'the baby continued to be somebody else'. Our teeth, we have to admit, are a lifelong problem. To Alice, in the earliest stages of her Wonderland adventures, it proved to be just as difficult to know who she really was, or who she might be were she to return to the 'other world'. 'If I like being that person, I'll come up,' she said; 'if not, I'll stay down here till I'm somebody else.' Our problem, alas, is not to be solved, we find, by liking to be this or that person, but by discovering as best we may, and learning to live with, the person we are. Nor is it just a matter of explanation. 'I can't explain myself, I'm afraid, Sir,' said Alice, 'because I'm not myself, you see.' 'I don't see,' said the Caterpillar.

Alice was not alone with her problem. She was in the unseen but distinguished company of the Psalmist and Shakespeare, Wordsworth and poor John Clare, Kant and Heidegger, who at various times had asked just such questions and marvelled at the pathos and mystery of man's being. She was also in that much greater company of innumerable nameless human beings whose harsh, hard, bitter conditions of life had wrung from them obstinate questionings to which prophets and teachers, law-givers and religious leaders, had attempted to give their answers. She was reflecting upon the most ancient problem of self-knowledge, upon the nature of reality, and we remember that in her case adventures did not end until she bravely denounced the frightening creatures that surrounded her as only a pack of cards, the pasteboard appearances of thrones and powers. The threatening monsters of the world of human history, whether conjured into being by reckless selfish violent men or encountered in the obdurate conditions of the natural world, are not so easily dispersed. Alice may be said to have epitomised in a remarkable way those difficulties of being human which now perplex the modern man, not least in the danger of being drowned in one's own tears. Her use of the word 'person' is a stroke of good fortune. Two generations later she would have called herself an individual and found it even more difficult to know how to set about being herself. She would have been still more bewildered to account for the variety of creatures who claimed to be her various selves. But being a wise little girl she clung to the word person, and it is with this word and what it stands for in human life today that spirituality must be as closely concerned with as possible. The Yes to God that we endeavour to make must be a personal Yes. The response that we make to ourselves and to others must be no less.

Why is it so important now? That we live in times of crisis, if not of catastrophe, is clear. Our increasingly urbanised world, the Vanity Fair of an erstwhile confident generation, looks more like the City of Destruction. Our major problem is to discern among the many threatening issues that now confront modern man, whether of war, racialism, pollution or starvation, what key question, if any, may be said to underlie them all, and what it is that, without giving way to a dangerous over-simplification, most clearly calls for recognition. It is hardly enough to walk through the streets crying 'Woe to the bloody city'. The word of the Gospel is a summons to men at such a time to look up, to expect to see, not easy answers certainly nor the blowing away of spectres, but evidence that God has not forsaken His people. His engagement with them still stands. The business of prayer is still to discern in what ways our response to that engagement is to be made. Prayer seeks to see where the mortice and tenon, the dovetailing of eternal and temporal things, has come awry, and how re-engagement in penitence and hope may be made. We pray in the first place to hear what the Spirit says to the churches and to everyman, to hear the questions which God puts to men, to feel the promptings of His hand, and that prophetic witness may not go unheeded.

To say that the crisis that we face is the crisis of the personal, as men like John MacMurray and Martin Buber among others have been saying for almost a generation, is to focus attention upon the spiritual issue so faced, upon the thing with which prayer is immediately concerned. For prayer is nothing if not a personal act of engagement with another, and in christian understanding it is from such engagement that the word itself emerged. The true pattern and the true fulfilment of human life were to be seen in the personal relationship which constituted the truth of God's being and in that truth becoming the way and the life of his creature man. What now makes it so much a matter of choice between life and death is the fact that for some centuries with increasing deliberation men have chosen to live and to shape their aggregate life with a disregard for the person and the personal. They have abolished and set aside obligations and ties of a social and cultural kind which once belonged to and ensured the continuance of an ordered corporate existence. The changes involved set men free to regard themselves as so many Robinson Crusoes to develop their islands as they wished and to deal with others as likewise free to accept or reject the terms they offered to them. The outcome of such liberation, while beneficent in many respects and able to extend the scope of human enterprise far beyond anything conceived of in an earlier age, has put in question the nature of society itself, straining it with cruel, violent and fearful movements, and giving rise to panic-stricken efforts to impose a social cohesion upon its turbulent constituents. But the conception of man's life as the life of the individual has held its place, and so accustomed are the majority of people to speaking of themselves as individuals that they find it pedantic and awkward to be asked to attend to the personal. Personalities are outstanding individuals, to get personal is to invade the privacy of the individual, and to receive personal attention is to be singled out for special treatment. Men do not connect the grave problems which endanger human welfare and survival with choice or discrimination in their conceptions of man, still less with the nature of the relation of man with God. Religion itself, once seen as the most inclusive corporate expression of human life, took on in the modern world an increasingly privatised character and lost much of its power to appeal to or speak in terms of a common mind and a common life. The subjective aspect of spirituality tended to overshadow all else, so that to speak of the personal as 'the great cardinal fact in a universe that is advancing towards maximum unity' or as 'the particular centre of divinisation' or the 'mesh of the cosmos', could not but be regarded as unfamiliar language in such a world.

A self which does not receive its character and direction from the eternal is already lost. A world of such selves is a lost world. The process of individualisation must in the end dissolve all ties, disavow all responsibility and reduce communication to something akin to traffic direction on a motorway. The individual is going where he wants to go. He is an entity by himself, for himself and of himself. He may glory in being himself alone or he may choose to exercise his individual right to co-operate with others for just such purposes as may gratify or fulfil his individual desires and needs. He may affect for his self-protection a nationalistic or civic code of behaviour. If he chooses 'to go it alone', to regard others as simply the means to his self-advancement, to interpret all questions from the angle of his self-satisfaction, he may be disliked or feared but he cannot on the individualistic grounds that he and others have chosen to stand on be seriously challenged. If like Shylock he stands upon his bond in a society that admits no other responsibility between man and man than that which is there agreed upon, he must have his pound of flesh. He is doing what he thinks fit with his own. 'True is what is mine.'

This looks like the oversimplification that we spoke of earlier. Our society knows in practice a great deal more of interdependence in its working life than any that have gone before. It organises its millions in teams and shifts and institutions, and for its working purposes it has begun to treat the world as a single field of resources and enterprise. A common workshop and a common market are already within sight. It is only when we examine the nature of the assumptions acted upon and the extent to which organisation is the only effective common factor that the issue of the personal and its bearing upon spirituality becomes a vital matter. Human life in its increasingly crowded condition needs organisation for a great many aspects of its well-being. The life of a great city is inconceivable without it. But organisation can do no more than put men and goods into certain places. It is the servant of certain assumptions about the nature of men and their good life. It usurps the place of the divine when it hides from men the engagement with God that has pronounced them to be His people and related them to one another as members of one body, when it ignores or denies the transcendent element in each man, and imposes its own categorisation upon their lives. What

Buber calls 'politicisation', the treatment of all human affairs from the angle of reasons of state, follows swiftly upon the ousting of all claims but those of the individual. Individuals can only be organised, and if human beings be no more than this then organisation is God. Religions must give it pride of place, concern themselves chiefly with social cohesion such as the time demands, and permit the State to take over the functions of a church. The growth of the omni-competent state has kept pace with the loss of a sense of the personal and the fragmentation of the structures of traditional communities, substituting its organised forms and planned control for as much of personal relationship as it could grasp and reducing the ties within society to those which power and technology require. The collective rather than the community becomes the pattern approved for social life. The Hobbesian dream takes flesh, proclaims itself 'a multitude of men made One Person', and to make quite clear the nature of this substitute person, insists that it find its unity, not in the represented nor in God but in the Representer, the Leviathan itself. Organisation man comes into his own.

Individualism thus comes full circle to a collectivism that cannot afford to tolerate deviation. It is not deterred from dealing with dissenters in inhuman and degrading ways for it is itself the outcome of a depersonalised conception of man's nature. The alienation of man from man and the reduction of human beings to economic tools to which Feuerbach and Marx drew attention become the premise of political action, and for the Yes to God there is substituted a periodic demand for a Yes of approval from the subjects of the organisation. Bigger and more vociferous assemblies of the organised become a feature of politicised life. The shout is its public prayer.

It is not difficult to persuade oneself that this picture is too bad to be true, or to point to the innumerable examples of kindly, humane and community-conscious behaviour which our social life affords. Nevertheless the warning has been fearfully explicit. The price of neglect and indifference is Auschwitz. To lose sight of the person, to ignore the claims of personal responsibility, to foster the Eichmann interpretation of public duty, is to enter upon that process of human reductionism in which men shrink human heads for ornaments, take human skin for lampshades and film the agonies of men being slowly strangled for the amusement of the subject population. That mankind has come this far upon the road to the rejection of personhood indicates the nature of the crisis to be faced. What was exposed to view in the concentration camp operations was not the ancient brutality of men or the savage determination to do away with enemies as speedily as possible, but the sophisticated attempt to explore the possibilities of human degradation, to discover how the personal features of human life could be defaced. It was the choice of a No to a meaningful notion of life.

We come then to the question of personhood alerted by such horrific signs, but standing no less in need of seeing in much less repellent forms in the conventional usages of our everyday world the rejection of the personal, in the life of the Church as in that of secular society. The sect-type churches have, throughout history, borne their witness to the need to struggle to keep the personal relationships of brothers-in-Christ and fellow-heirs of the kingdom from being displaced and overridden by others of hierarchical, political and organisational character. Neither they nor the great churches have been as watchful as their Lord warned them to be, for such watchfulness as He coupled with prayer is not simply observation of what appears to be going on – the trial of an unknown political prisoner or the destruction of a people whom nobody has ever heard of – but radical doubt and questioning of what is being taken for granted in the social order that obtains. A church called christian, remembering the Son of Man exposed to ridicule, degradation and death, must always be asking who this is that is thus mocked, imprisoned, deprived and thrust from sight. Things all too easily go unperceived because men simply do not want to see.

Such a critique continually kept alert is as important a part of prayer as the research which Teilhard de Chardin so justly described as adoration. Without it, penitence loses its reality. Our proneness to sin takes the form, as often as not, of simply doing and thinking what the rest of society thinks and does, of accepting the relationships which obtain in the political and social order we grew up in, of failing to note the changes going on within it. Entering upon the vast technological revolution of today, men have even more need than before to notice the extent to which in the industrialisation of society the personal element is submerged beneath an arrangement of life designed primarily to produce more goods, more power and more profit. The fetish of commodities – 'only what you haven't got is desirable' – reduced the relationships of human beings to those of hands and employers of hands, machine minders and machines, whose worth could be measured in terms of money. How religiously such reductionism was carried out and received may be seen in a single episode described by Dickens in *Dombey and Son*, a book which plays upon the theme of sonship – unto us a son is born – with a grim comment upon human hopes and christian faith. The child, Paul Dombey, suddenly asks his father what money is. Mr Dombey, whose whole life is devoted to making money, is, like a religious enthusiast suddenly asked to explain his faith, momentarily confused. He makes an effort to explain bullion and credit and other such features of the financial world. The child brushes all this aside and repeats his question. 'What is money? What can it do?' Mr Dombey is now recovered and well able to confess his faith. 'Money,' he staunchly replies, 'money can do anything.'

To speak of persons and the personal is to take the discussion of man's life and nature to the source of his being, to the Yes of God that permits him to be. Whatever we say of him must be derived from our faith in Him from whom our sense of personhood springs, from whose addressing of Himself to man in revelation the I–Thou relationship is made known. Our Yes to God cannot be made realistically save in the terms which we believe Him to have chosen, in the channels and speech of the people's life that He has called into this area of communication. The personal is the response through which we acknowledge the faith we hold in being so addressed. Hebrew and christian spirituality alike start from an affirmation of this divine concern: 'A Syrian ready to perish was my father', and continue in a deepening perception of the unchanging compassionate regard of the Father for His children. Such spirituality does not blur the distinction between divine and human, but insists that the miracle of personal intercourse lies in the relating of the two, steadily approaching the sense of the personal in order to give adequate expression to its faith. For the Hebrew assertion that the 'Lord God is between me and thee for ever', and for the christian the words of Jesus Himself – 'as thou, Father, art in me, and I in Thee, that they also may be one in us', come as close as human language can come to indicating the personal relationship. It is understood as intentional activity directed towards the achievement of an ever-deepening communion, a seeking to know the other at the most intimate level of being.

In the meanwhile we face the question of self-knowledge. 'Your essential duty and desire,' wrote Teilhard de Chardin, 'is to be united with God. But in order to be united, you must first of all be yourself as completely as possible.' It is here that the element of passion enters into such a prospective engagement, here the mystery of the self is most painfully apprehended, for it is in the experience of having nothing of one's self that the truth of personhood begins to be known. Like the younger son of Christ's parable we have to come to ourselves in our destitution and frustration. It is in this condition that we experience the need for a word that expresses as adequately as possible the self that we begin to perceive ourselves to be, a word that acknowledges that we are 'no-thing' and that in our 'no-thingness' we encounter the mystery of our being. We need a word that allows for the uniqueness known to the consciousness within us, which permits growth and change to take place without loss of identity, which can if need be contemplate rebirth and resurrection, which relates us in intimate fashion to others, and which distinguishes between the reality and the falsehood which attends upon our behaviour in the world. We need such a word above all to describe the one who prays, the nature of the oneness of the one who prays and the character of prayer itself. Prayer must be becoming more and more meaningless and impossible to make in a world in which the personal is being set aside or deliberately destroyed.

This looks indeed as if we require a portmanteau word that would have made Humpty-Dumpty's efforts look trivial, but as christians came to it they were struggling to say something which does outdistance all other attempts to put truth into words. They were trying to speak of God. The use to which we now put the word in relation to spirituality rests firmly on the choice made in christian theology to thus speak of God and thereafter of human beings made in His image. It was not the first nor would it be the last time that human language was stretched to breaking point by such a task. The attempt verges on the ludicrous and has often been mocked. It is easy to forget that the circumstances in which the attempts were made were not speculative exercises but protracted efforts to deal with human experience, to put into words that which men had seen and heard, to be honest and truthful about it. Their very inadequacy confesses their recognition of that which must for ever break through language and escape. They were struggling to 'describe' the godhead and the dealings of God with mankind, to express their faith in God whom the heaven of heavens could not contain but who nevertheless dwelt among men and made their bodies the temple of His Holy Spirit, who Himself pure Spirit took flesh and was made very man of a human mother. The immensity of their task is clear. They came up with the word person, awkwardly conceived then, greatly neglected since, but desperately needed now if the Yes that we are trying to make to God in the world today is to have any life of its own. Person sums up both our human predicament and our hope in God.

What Western christian theologians did was to take the word used for the actor's mask through which in classical theatre he declaimed his lines, and used it to mean not a mask to be put on, a part to be assumed, a role to be played, but the truth of being, whether of God or man. They stopped short of saying that God is a person, but they spoke of a life in Him in which personality expressed the unity and diversity by which the divine was made known to man. They proclaimed God's Yes of revelation in terms of the Blessed Trinity, a holy community of Persons, in whom 'none is afore, or after other; none is greater, or less than another'. Persons, they affirmed, were persons in community, inconceivable in isolation from each other yet distinguishable in their peculiar glory, in such communion of fellowship and love that perfect unity of being remained their essential nature. Persons were never alone – 'I am not alone,' He said, 'for I know that Thou hearest me always,' and prayer was that intercommunication between such persons so joined together. The creative act that permitted all things to be was the personal act of the Triune God. Revealing and restoring flowed no less from the nature of the personal.

Such teaching sprang from the honest attempt of the christian Church to present as faithfully as possible the experience from which its own life was derived and what it had known of life lived out in response to that Trinitarian pattern. It was deterred neither by the theoretical nor the practical difficulties of attempting to say Yes to God in this fashion. Spirituality today must do no less and it is for this reason that the battle for the person and the personal is so important. A doctrine which purports to speak of the absolute mystery that is at the heart of all it believes and knows is in great danger of becoming no doctrine at all if it cannot be rooted and grounded and perpetually rediscovered in the everyday life of men and women, in the heartfelt knowledge of those who confess such a faith. If such be the meaning of secularised knowledge, then secularisation must be the constant movement of the spirit at work. It must be for ever emptying itself, as He emptied Himself, of such glory as might separate it from that which it loves. The Passion is the putting off of all things that the divine engagement may be entire, a secularisation of the eternal that creatures of time might inherit eternal life. Prayer must continually reground itself therefore to speak that which we know from our personal life.

Preparation for prayer is bound for this reason to be greatly concerned with the kind of life that churches and religious communities are actually living, with the relationships of persons within them, remembering that we are not ourselves if we try to step out of or leave behind these societies when we pray. Our job in constant preparation is to be learning to see, and the elucidation of prayer takes us back to the beginning of it over and over again, the marvellous flashes of goodness and the terrible failures of personal rapport that are intermingled in the life of these societies we belong to. Judgement does and must ever begin with the house of God. It is here that huckstering can be most truly rapacious, and the hurt that ensues most deadly. If the personal means something less than, and in all too many cases hardly anything of, the mystery of God made manifest in human life, it is to the absence of the experience of true community in the life of the churches and religious bodies that this must be traced. Sin can have no more deadly expression than in putting asunder persons and thus blocking up all the channels through which their lives as people of God should be nurtured. Yet it is this which all too often is left to take care of itself so that the common life in the body of Christ is there in name only, and the praying men do is a solitary thing, weakened by lack of personal involvement with others. All too often structures are being relied on to do duty for the true interpenetration of lives. Congregations and fellowships are all too often aggregations of people who never get any nearer to speaking a common language growing in a common mind, acting with common purpose and praying in one spirit. Their members are just as exposed to depersonalisation as those who remain outside them and make no professions of faith in a unifying Spirit and a Body of Christ. Priority in discipleship must lie in deliberate seeking of ways to assemble such bodies of people to find out together what personal relationships mean. Only so does the great inheritance of Trinitarian faith become for each member of them a truly liberating and energising force.

Hebrew spirituality prepared the ground for such understanding of the personal, and much of the lack of concern for the Old Testament among christian people today is bound up with a lack of understanding of its relevance in these terms. It insisted in the first place upon the feature of choice, whether of a nation, a prophet or a disciple, to make clear that the operations of divine activity are best understood in terms of personal intention. With often desperate intensity of pain it read that personal intention into and out of its experience, compelled thereby to search for the implications in response to God of what had taken place. It found its answer in love, and it described the nature of that love in the detailed obligations of moral righteousness, of mercy, generosity, humility and justice. Unwillingly at times, and always with shortcomings, it recognised that such singularity of choice in no way impeded universality of intention. The personal so conceived of could begin to apprehend how all time and space could be narrowed down to the compass of one human life in and through which the eternal Lord God would make manifest His will.

This is but a beginning. Personal choice looks for personal response, and it is in the moments when a man sweats and trembles at the prospect of the choice which he himself must make that the Yes to God is formed. It is not just a matter of submission, of bowing to what God does. The God of Abraham chooses and commands, but he will not hide from His chosen servant that which He proposes to do. The personal is not that which is done over a man's head. A man is asked to take to heart and make his own the things of God. It is the beginning of something described as friendship. God is said to talk with Abraham as a man talks with his friend, and on this footing God questions, replies, reasons and pleads with men in order that they may learn to answer for themselves and do so with an increasing understanding of what they are called upon to do. Man's dependence upon God remains throughout, but the whole nature of that dependence is seen with new eyes as the personal aspect grows clearer. In such a relationship between persons the element of trust permits the answering Yes to be shaped in perfect freedom. Servanthood gives place to friendship, and the Passion involved in such engagement finds its most poignant expression in the face to face encounter of Jesus with Judas in the Garden of Gethsemane with the words 'Friend, wherefore art thou come?' The divine initiative seeks to elicit from the loved friend that truth without which the reality of personhood cannot be known, but which also affirms that nothing whatever can break its intentional love.

This Biblical understanding of man's life does not begin as so much of contemporary thinking begins with the separate existence of men and women but with those relationships which envelop them throughout life. It sees them not as restrictions upon the freedom of an individual but as the conditions for the well-being and enhancement of life. It uses the experience of family ties and national membership together with the notions of the body and buildings, however limited and defective these may be, to express the full sense of incorporation, sustaining and relatedness that holds up each life to stand before God. It is this awareness of inclusion carried to its final stages which strikes the most jubilant note in the New Testament. The person has come to the truth of his being in that inclusion. 'If any man be in Christ, he is a new creature . . . you are all one in Christ Jesus . . . none of us liveth unto himself and no man dieth unto himself, for whether we live, we live unto the Lord, and whether we die, we die unto the Lord . . . for by One Spirit are we all baptized into one Body . . . and ye are the Body of Christ and members in particular.' Growing up in such an inclusive life, a man could not but be aware that it surpassed all other experiences of participation and fulfilment. It is a note not entirely absent from the experience of men and women today but one that stands in need of continual renewal. If indeed the charismatic movements and the search for commitment for liberation for the oppressed peoples of the world can restore to christians such a sense of community they will have done much to make possible a Yes to God from the modern world. In the meanwhile that personal relation that belongs to the smaller community of marriage is nowhere better expressed than by two painters, one of whom, John Constable, is said to have addressed his wife as 'My dearest life', and the other, Stanley Spencer, writing to his wife Hilda after parting from her: 'Not having you in my life is like going back to time after once living in eternity . . . Nothing is real me that is not Hilda-me.'

It is this experience of such open fearless loving face to face relationship that gives full meaning to the personal, which constitutes the Yes made by one person to another, and which those who know of it would seek to extend to others. We can see it in the flesh wherever such acceptance happens. It is one of the most moving experiences of life to watch a bewildered frightened human being, starved of friendship and hardly daring to be expectant of it, blossom out into a happy, trustful and confident personal life as the result of being so welcomed and received. It is of the essence of the Gospel that we are so received in Christ, that His Yes to men is pronounced in such directly personal terms. Human beings like Nathanael and Philip, Nicodemus and Zaccheus, the woman of Samaria and the man born blind, are pictured as those faced abruptly by a personal intervention to which they respond with something like a gulp of astonishment. It is not simply that they had never been addressed like this before, though that was noticed and felt, but that they realised that it was the singularity of their life and being that was being marked. 'Whence knowest thou me?' It is the kind of noticing in its various forms upon which Shakespeare dwells in *Much Ado about Nothing*. Incarnate love in the Person of Jesus Christ noticed men and women in this way. We in our learning to say Yes to God are required to approach each other as apprentices to the mystery of personal recognition, to take infinite trouble to grow into it, and to know within ourselves the transfiguring outcome of being sought out and known in this way. The light in which the reality of human life is thus seen is the presence itself, the Shekinah that has approached and filled the area of meeting with its revealing splendour. Before ever words are spoken, and beyond any words that may be uttered, those included in it know that they are loved.

Men are nevertheless slow and fearful in respect of the personal. Not all those who met Jesus Christ met on such ground. His sternest, saddest condemnation was made of men of great apparent religious devotion whose piety was a mask. That they prayed much led Jesus to comment in parable fashion upon the kind of prayer that such play-acting gave rise to. It turned not only fellowmen but God Himself into an audience before whom the play was played, and claimed approval and applause for its appearance of devotion. Personal relationship was excluded and the great channel of apprehending the truth in life choked with a self-regarding deceit. Surrendered to the business of 'seeming', such men became so fearful of having the mask torn away, that they moved quickly to destroy the person who confronted them.

Personhood ascribed to the Holy Trinity implies that the relation within that Holy Community are such that perfect freedom, understanding, love and mutual involvement, a total Yes, obtain throughout eternity. Personhood for human beings is personhood in the making, the responsive Yes to fellowmen and to the cosmos itself in whose company and creative drives the nurturing process is carried on. The idea of cornering things for ourselves alone or becoming self-made men becomes a ludicrous affair. We cannot cultivate a private version of personal life for personhood is a recognition of total indebtedness on the one hand and total requiredness on the other. Prayer must keep before us that polarity since individualised worldliness hates to acknowledge indebtedness and affects to despise requiredness. Prayer must for ever remind us that we have nothing that we did not receive. It must go further and enable us to treat what we have received as 'gifts' and to acknowledge our relationship with the giver. Giving and receiving in personal fashion make up the web and woof of our existence. To assert the primacy of the personal in life is to welcome the never-to-be-exhausted enrichment that is made possible by unconditional giving.

Personhood so conceived as the truth of our growing up in Christ involves us as we have said in every struggle to end the oppressions and deceits which hinder that growth in the world of men. To live and to pray in a personal way must mean a lifelong struggle against whatever expresses contempt or hatred or indifference to men and women of any kind. It means identification with the despised, not because they are better people than those who ill-treat them or are welcoming to those who endeavour to help them, but simply because they are needed and needy. A mankind broken up into various 'worlds', superpowers and backward peoples, immigrants, refugees, displaced persons, ruling and servant classes, is a world shouting No to God, as Scott's Black Dwarf cried out, "Common humanity! where got ye that catchword – that noose for woodcocks – that common disguise for mantraps – that bait which the wretched idiot who swallows will soon find covers a hook with barbs ten times sharper than those you lay for the animals which you murder for your luxury.' A world of segregated peoples must inevitably become a world of retarded persons, fearful and anxious to defend themselves against whatever might make demands upon them, absorbed in manufacturing for themselves a clear and unambiguous self-image, making a mask to cover the face of the human being. Where hell is other people, where the world of fantasy is preferred to that of reality, where purity means no contact with the other, the personal withers and the Yes to God dies away.

But our time is a time of expectation and hope. It is now fifty years since Martin Buber spoke clearly of the significance of the I–Thou relationship, insisting upon the need to recognise the sphere of the 'between' or interhuman, pleading for the rebirth of dialogue, patiently explaining the meaning of the crisis of communication and urging men to look for the new theophany in the night of their desperation. Waves of evil have not silenced that voice nor drowned that expectation. In strange fashion Hopkins' poem 'The Wreck of the Deutschland' with its great affirmative cry,

> *I did say yes*
> *O at lightning and lashed rod;*
> *Thou heardst me truer than tongue confess*
> *Thy terror, O Christ, O God;*

had anticipated the storm and sounded a profounder note than that of *Ulysses*, 'The Waste Land' and the literature of the post-war mood. Buber's voice is now one of a great chorus, 'since we have been a conversation and have been able to hear from one another ... we are soon song', and the world is full of such voices, of Bonhoeffer and John XXIII, Teilhard de Chardin and Martin Luther King, Péguy and Gutierrez, Ernst Bloch and Pablo Neruda, and a multitude of others, so that to speak of the pentecostal experience is not to talk of something outside the mainstream of human awareness today or of a peculiar form of spirituality, but to acknowledge what is most living in the response of mankind. Although we are but at the beginning of understanding what the encounter of dialogue means, recognition of the necessity laid upon christians to speak openly and personally with the world, with other faiths, with other disciplines, of the need to learn what can only be communicated in silence, of the task of going out to the estranged, has brought mankind to a new attentiveness to the concordant discord through which a new Yes to God may be spoken. The personal is known in the increasing recognition, freed from fear of interdependence, knitting together the whole company of mankind. We can understand a little better why Jesus Christ spoke of the stones crying out for we have at last learned to listen to them. We can begin to follow what Teilhard de Chardin meant in speaking of the whole ascending scale of creation in personal terms. In *Le Milieu Divin*, Teilhard draws a picture of a moment in his life, when, taking a lamp he descended into the depths of his being as if he were a cave-explorer going down into the darkness, discovering at each new level new aspects of his personal life, until at last he stood halted, as the explorer so often is, upon the brink of a dark river swirling away into the abyss. It is a profoundly moving picture of confrontation with the mystery of one's life, but, more important, it points further. Returning to the world of everyday affairs and social engagement, he saw that here too the same mystery of personal life was disclosed in the huge intricate complex of circumstance, in the convergent processes that informed the consciousness, in the reflection and the responsiveness which shaped the human Yes to the creative act of God. Inner and outer life were so interwoven with that myriad number of forces at work that the personal might be seen as the growing tip of its grand design, consciously participating in it and adding its own unique contribution. As the finite variety of the creaturely unfolded itself to the eyes and mind of the inquirer, so the scope of the personal might be perceived in its true glory, awakening to and embracing them 'for all things are yours, and you are Christ's, and Christ is God's'.

It was a like experience that Franz Rosenzweig described when he spoke of his decision to remain a Jew. He had found himself for some years poised upon the brink of a choice between Judaism and christianity. There came a day when, in his own words, he too descended into the vaults of his own being to face the supreme problem of his spiritual life. He came back to the light of common day, not simply with the decision made, but with a new sense of the commonness of the day, a new awareness of the nature of his engagement with the world of men, of the world to be redeemed into personality, of his own relationship with the students and waiters and barbers' apprentices as persons-in-the-making like himself. New depths in the divine had been disclosed in this new perception of the world at work. The interior life was no private world detached from or more real than the world of circumstance and history but entry into that dimension where the personal engagement of God with His worlds and creatures might be known.

The personal then is that focus of all the inter-relatedness that gives to each of us our particular place in God's world. When we strive to know ourselves, we are seeking to know not a speck of dust nor the species man but the Word that was spoken and took our flesh, the Yes that permitted us to be. We are seeking to know it because we are sought-out, because we are named as persons are named, because to be persons at all is to find in our hearts the Yes that strives to reply. We are that Yes, not of ourselves alone, but in Him and by Him and through Him in eternity.

8 *Beginning to Pray Again*

'To pray. To pray that a whole people be spared from falling among the dead souls, the dead peoples, the dead nations. Be spared from falling down dead, Be spared from becoming a dead people, a dead nation. Be spared from mildew. Be spared from going rotten in spiritual death, in the earth, in hell.'
Charles Péguy, *The Mystery of the Charity of Joan of Arc.*

TRY TO FOLLOW THOSE WORDS OF PÉGUY; TRY TO CONCEIVE their intensity, feel their burden of anguish, see their relevance to our human condition in the world today. Men and nations can go dead and rot in spiritual death. We do not have to subscribe to the theories of a Vico, a Spengler, a Toynbee, to account for this. We can smell death in our modern world if we are alive to what is happening in it, just as we can choose between life and death in the choices we make every day of our lives. The Bible, of course, is full of warnings about it, and texts have been freely, much too freely, quoted to impress men about the need to repent. But what God did to Shiloh only becomes a message of real importance to us when we begin to see where these choices that we make or permit to be made in our name bear fruit, when prayer itself throws light upon the outcome of our choices. 'So foolish was I, and ignorant,' lamented the Psalmist, realising that culpability lay chiefly in a quite pitiful edging away from anything like a Yes to God, a blurring of vision and speech that left unexamined and unexpressed the things that were there to be noticed, a multitude of trivial evasions that diverted attention from the great issues to be faced, a lack of will to bring together the insights and intimations that were there to be utilised. Our Yes to God has got to embrace this world, our world, by the most patient attention to the immediate if minute demands it makes upon us. We must be awake enough to respond.

Try to sense the desperate reaching out of Péguy's words and follow their reiteration, not as a repetition of words only, but as a renewal of effort, as the anguished movement of one who wrestles for life, and hear them as something wrung not only from the lips that murmur them but from the heart of one 'whose sweat was as it were great drops of blood falling down to the ground'. Prayer is not always made at such extremities, but whether we marvel at God's glories in silence, shout with delight at His mercies or weep in pain and misery, it draws on the strength of passion and engages us once again in what God is about. Péguy put those words into the mouth of a nun to whom the young Joan of Arc went to pour out her grief for the state of her land and people. Péguy himself prayed often like that because he knew that not only his beloved France but the far wider world stood in desperate need of such praying. Péguy died sixty years ago but we know now how greatly we stand in need of going on and going further with that prayer. The condition of human life has not grown simpler in the intervening years but the spiritual issues have begun to be presented in starker terms; crises have given intimations of Crisis.

Try to live with those words even for a short time; try to come back to them often. They have acquired a deeper relevance in the intervening years. They are spoken again, for example, in all that Thomas Merton said about monasticism needing to be open to the social reality of the twentieth century, about the christian contemplative's need to seek the most living participation on the events of the world. They are spoken in sharp demanding tones by Gustavo Gutierrez on behalf of a submerged world. They have been spoken in every language by the poets and artists we have spoken of earlier, by Klee and Picasso, by Solzhenitsyn and Neruda, by Brecht and Freire. They are being spoken wherever men and women go that extra mile as 'burden-bearers of creation', taking it on themselves to make some acts of reparation and reconciliation or giving themselves generously to patient service of others. Much of the endeavour to say Yes to God today must take the form of learning to see how pitifully small has been the concern of the christian Church for great areas of human life, how little it has understood or even supposed that it was called upon to try to understand what was being done to the bodies and minds of human beings in the great political, economic and scientific revolutions that have changed the map of human existence. We said at the beginning that prayer is prayer for enlightenment; it means praying as Solomon did for an understanding heart. One of the most eloquent passages in modern literature is the sermon preached over the body of a dead Negro in James Baldwin's novel *Another Country*. The climax comes with the words, 'Don't let it make you bitter, try to understand. Try to understand. The world's already bitter enough, we got to try to be better than the world.' Being better than the world at the present time starts from experiencing the pain of being in the world as a personal thing, particularising it in the details of what it means to be this man or that woman, seeing such things as parts of the Passion, taking the engagement that is offered in them in an unembittered spirit, pursuing in all things the coming to be of a world which in all its enterprises honours the Incarnate Lord. All too often we have failed to see the vision of God because we have not wanted to look in the directions and circumstances in which He chooses to present Himself to His people.

Try to feel the force of those words before we turn to our own efforts to pray. Péguy's style, in prose and poetry, shocked great numbers of his fastidious countrymen who thought it clumsy, turgid and wearisome. Words seemed to be used like hammers beating out in monotonous fashion a heavy rhythm, slow and exacting like the rhythms of the earth. It was left to a few more discerning friends to appreciate their truth. One called it 'a rhythmic footstep', the plodding place of a peasant as he foots out a heavy journey. Another likened it in style to the ancient litanies whose observations were like stones in a desert, each so like the other yet just a little different, each establishing to the patient eye a difference to be underlined, insisted upon, repeated seemingly, emphasised for its difference and made the measure of the attention of continuing prayer. This is not 'vain repetition' but continual new effort, geared to an awareness of the length of the journey. It is not the only way of praying but it is the one which most of us have need to learn just because great tracts of life are only going to be lived through at such a pace. As Tristram Shandy's father remarked upon hearing that St Maxima had lain in the tomb two centuries before her canonisation, ''Tis but a slow rise, Brother Toby, in this self-same army of martyrs!'

The point is that each of us has to find for himself the rhythmical pace at which he can keep going in his prayers, each of us has to learn to change step on occasion and alter the pace when the time for some change comes round. Do it too often and you begin to stumble and falter. Fail to change step when needed and you run out of breath and stop. Much of praying consists in saying old words in a way that makes them new, in refusing to let them go dead by treating them as if they were not able to be new words. This is not a mechanical view of praying but in truth its opposite, taking note of our make-up, age, condition of body and mind, and all the circumstances in which we live. People in bodily pain, in tension of mind, in old age, in uprooted conditions, have all to be helped to be changing their step. We have to find the pace that is truly our own, and not regret that we cannot skip along as once we could. It may be a much slower pace than we'd care to admit to, one that seems to make no headway at all, one that possesses few virtues but the chief merit of keeping on. Sometimes, no doubt, we can all pray like Gerard Manly Hopkins' verse 'all in a rush with richness', sometimes we shall have to grope our way like 'cavers' in a dark, disagreeable tunnel where 'time is stalactite'. All this is part of the process of learning to know ourselves in the only terms that matter, the terms of one who intends to go on to the end. We must find for ourselves the words to go with the pace, both old and new ones. The words we take with us now, the words that imagination fits to the journey itself, don't have to be defended. If they have to be bitten through as once men bit coins to try their metal, then it's up to us to bite hard and spit out the words that won't stand the test. We are not to be hypnotised by words either, however sublime they sound or sacred their ancestry, and least of all by the specialised talk of experts in their own various fields of knowledge. In prayer as in good writing the style's the man, and we must by much labour find our own, drawing upon the common language of the people of God, our mother tongue, and shaping our own authentic Yes with it in virtue of what we have seen and heard. All of which sends us back once again to that life prior to prayer, for our business is not to invent a peculiar song of our own or make do with a hotch-potch of scraps got from others, but to discover what our part in the song of the earth, the music of the spheres, the Lord's song and the hymn of creation really amounts to and give it utterance. To adapt a phrase of Keats, if the prayer doesn't come naturally it had better not come at all, but naturally means both aspects of passion worked hard and engagement accepted with as much courage as we can bring to it.

I have chosen to begin this last chapter with Péguy's words for a number of reasons. All of them having to do with kinds of praying that our sense of joy and pain bound up together constrain us to try to do. All of them have to do with the world, for though it is true that the engagement began before we got here, before ever the worlds were made, and will continue after they have ceased to be, it is this world that for the present defines our job. That job is to be good human beings, to find out what that means for ourselves and others, not to treat the world as a back-cloth to a solo performance nor to try to forget it whenever we try to pray. The world is the givenness of things we have to make use of but it is also God's much loved world towards which, for that reason, we cannot be indifferent or neglectful or hostile. The Yes that we want to make must be made in all that He claims for His body, for our christian faith is in One who willed that nothing be lost, and its peculiar joy lies in its trust that even time can be redeemed. So the claim for His Body must be as wide as the heavens and the earth, must embrace the one and the many, eternity and time, spirit and matter, male and female, hiddenness and revelation, joy and sorrow. It must comprehend the particularities of all created things, the uses made of them, and the unity that approves and glories in their diversity. We are to pray, no matter how hidden the inmost room from which it is made as those who are, up to their full capacity, to grow in wonder and delight at the vast context of God's action. We are to pray, no matter how still our bodies, as those who are sustained by the great tidal wave of His oncoming Kingdom. We are to pray, no matter how silent our lips, as those who join in the dawn-chorus of a new creation.

So, help in praying is not a matter of producing a pattern-book from which others can choose the style they favour, but much more an indication of what has meant much to one in the hope that it may encourage others to do far better. There is bound to be an incompleteness and an unspoken element in it. As Péguy's Joan of Arc said to God, 'I dare to have a secret with you.' Fr Delp, whose prison meditations have the dimensions of an enormous room, himself spoke of a creative dialogue into which God in secret draws both men and women, continuing in this way His own creative purpose.

It is difficult to begin with any one aspect of such prayer without giving the impression that this is the primary thing or the place from which others should start. Much better to see it as a sphere from any point on the surface of which any of us makes the journey into the interior. Somewhere the different lines of approach converge; always we can be aware of the alternative routes. At all times we have need to be ready to make use of several of these approaches, and not to be imprisoned in them. Offices, spiritual exercises, methods of mental prayer, litanies, all have their place, and their function is to bring us into touch with the activity of the Spirit of God, the initiator of the cosmic purpose, the fiery energy of its unfolding, but we must not be tied to any of them. The whole point of prayer being personal and ourselves being persons is that while we owe everything we have to others and should be joyfully conscious of this, what we do with it must be ours by intention and not a copying of anyone else. To be personal is to be adding something to the diversity and the unity of the creation. It must likewise welcome, expect, make possible and cherish what others do and are.

There are certain features of our life which give us common ground, if we so choose to use them, for common prayer. There are others which sharply divide us, and we have suggested already that such indulgence of individualisation brings us to ruin and death. To an extent we do not often realise, our acceptance of social distinctions and divisions has gone far to make our acknowledgement of things common an almost private affair. What we share in are the events and experiences which cause us to exclaim with delight or pain or penitence or grief. They are those which remind us of our indebtedness, of requiredness, of the precariousness of life, of things humanly precious, ineffable, of final mystery. What divides us springs from style of life, education, tradition, wealth, sheer ignorance, as well as from different religious and philosophical backgrounds. The kind of help that we may try to give each other must take notice of this and not pretend that the divisions do not go very deep. Behind us lie centuries of persecution, and christians all too easily forget that this hideous thing practised in the name of Christ has left its own evil legacy of bitterness and distrust that affects the spiritual health of the world today. Péguy was right in seeing the Dreyfus affair as an instance of mildew and rottenness overtaking a nation. We need as much insight today to make clear that we do not escape such contamination merely by being ignorant of its sources. The prayer that affects to leave the world behind because it lacks the charity to face it is already so diseased, and its death a necessary condition of rebirth to a livelier faith.

To make our own personal steps in prayer, keeping the options open, looking for signs of common purpose, starting from that need to reply as honestly as we can to the questioning put to us from the Bible until today, we begin by looking at what this amounts to now. It demands attention to detail in observation. It is worth recalling von Hügel's advice to his niece about reading, even if it is going to be done on a much more limited scale than he would have thought of. Discrimination matters if men and women read no more than the newspaper, circulars and leaflets. Von Hügel was concerned that she should read not only widely but with careful method. She was to read with pencil in hand and mark on the inner and outer margins of a page the points of style and argument she noted, and she was to re-read to gain a grasp of the whole line of thought. It may sound laborious and pedantic, and we have to remind ourselves that this was preparation for prayer and not an attempt to make her a learned woman. If we are tempted to think that few people could or would make such efforts, we may well ask what the Church is for if not to assist and encourage each member of its company to do just this. Hebrew spirituality had never doubted that such reading and reflection upon reading was essential, that discussion on what was read was equally important and we can keep in mind Lenin's insistence that the job of a Bolshevik was to study and to study and to study. The Church has tended for too long to treat its members as if they were eternally infants, and the gaps between its learned and erudite scholars, its clergy and its rank and file members are a weakness and an embarrassment to any corporate action, and an impoverishing factor in its spirituality. So much prayer dwindles and dies because it has no solid foundation in reflection and shared understanding. This is to a great extent no more than another aspect of contemporary life in which almost all things conspire to push human life to a superficial level. An advertisement in *The Times* appeared as follows: 'Research shows that the average married couple have only 16 minutes of meaningful conversation together each week. How often does your husband talk to you? Is he more involved in hobbies, the telly, his work? Research writer, preparing thesis, is keen to hear case histories.' If communication in the basic community of life dwindles to such meagre proportions, if the communication within the parish churches gets absorbed in matters of finance, if communication within religious communities gets pushed a long way down the list of matters to be attended to, what chance is there that the common personal prayer of the people involved will grow rich by virtue of that which every member supplies? It is not the gross scandals that go far to corrupt the spiritual life of the churches so much as the low standards of corporate concern for the informing of the members about their real calling and common involvement.

What must be taken from von Hügel's advice in being deliberate over our praying amounts to learning to use a pencil and notebook our whole life through. When Péguy first produced his poem on Joan of Arc, the volume contained a great number of entirely blank pages. It was not a bad joke but an intimation that more was to come to fill out and deepen what had only been touched on so far. What we all need is a Book of Common Prayer, a Missal, a service book, with more blank pages than printed ones, an interleaved book in which we may write the things that are of personal weight and concern, in which we paste pictures or poems or fragments of letters, in which we note down the questions we find we must face. It is the work-book of our life, our attempt to relate those tremendous things of the Liturgy or the Psalms to the jobs and the problems and delights of our personal living. Children are often encouraged in schools today to make a prayer-book of their own like this. The pity is that we don't to any great extent take seriously enough the need to do this as adults, so that we dissipate rather than utilise our resources, and fail to hold our current experience within the field of the spirit long enough to permit the hallowing process to get under way. We need to be helped to annotate the Psalms or the Liturgy for ourselves with questions and comments that tie them to everyday life. The spiritual exercises that deepen devout apprehension within a particular tradition, like the Bible – study that pursues its internal cross-references as far as they go, need to be constantly re-engaged with living and corporate purpose. Our togetherness in common prayer should be the incentive to the most imaginative differentiation of our several spiritual lives.

The opening words of the First Epistle of St John are a good guide to this, for we have emphasised throughout this book that the need to see and be attentive to what we see at every turn is of primary importance. Our praying is to be underpinned with the perceived realities of our life in order that it may bear the weight of increasing engagement. St John's words, 'that which we have seen . . .' and 'we love because He loved us' make clear how the Yes of God and the Yes of men are bound together. Without the constant search for reality, begun in the first place by sustained effort to perceive the extent of our indebtedness to others and our completely recipient condition, spirituality tends to be overtaken by the search for certainties and authoritative safeguards on the one hand and by fantasy-making on the other. Both of these destroy the faith that praying is concerned to nurture, for with certainties we grow arrogant and with fantasies self-indulgent. People get lost in fantasy or crave for authoritative direction because they have not learned to note with gratitude the singular details of such goodness that comes their way. Genuine Yes to God cannot begin anywhere else:

> *I can no other answer make but thanks,*
> *And thanks and ever thanks.*

which sounds easy and natural enough when the heart is spontaneously overflowing with delight but which gets forgotten unless the perceptive attitude is being constantly renewed. Among all the great Biblical questions addressed to men which initiate a new level of dialogue and prepare the way for a Yes of greater content few penetrate more deeply to the personal level than that which follows the washing of the disciples' feet. 'Know ye what I have done to you?' It could be said that all prayer is occupied with answering that question. The attempted Yes must needs embrace all mankind and all that faith in God holds on to. If we relate it moreover to that far-off scene of Joseph standing before his brothers in Egypt saying, 'You thought to have done me evil, but God sent me before you to save your life', we see how the engagement with God and men is woven into a continuous theme which it is the business of prayer to return to as the sustaining truth of human life.

Some details of our map of prayer emerge from this. We shall not think of ourselves as called upon to say Yes to God unless we first hear the questions. In Yeats' words we have to

> *Bid Imagination run*
> *Much on the Great Questioner;*
> *What He can question, what if questioned I*
> *Can with a fitting confidence reply.*

It is an interrogative God with whom we have to do, and there can be no better exercise in the preparation for prayer than working through the Gospels to note every question that Jesus Christ is described as asking, and furthermore, seeing them as the culmination of a questioning which the writers of Genesis indicate as beginning in the garden and which continue to be put to men throughout the Old Testament record. Having learned to pay attention to these questions we shall be better able to ask the right questions ourselves. Our Yes to God goes astray all too often because either we grow inert and ask no questions at all, which is a poor reply to God who made us in His image, or we ask foolish inept questions which show that we haven't listened to His. To be good witnesses we have got to learn to get the questions right; otherwise we shall substitute our own version and be content with that.

The second feature can be described as compiling our own Benedicite, with the help of all those referred to earlier as openers of men's eyes and ears. We have now a long enough record of art and literature to see – as the Bible itself makes plain – that no statement, no style, no interpretation, is ever complete and finished. Alert preparation for prayer is therefore alive to the fact that our Yes to God stands in just such need of being restated. It is this, for example, that makes the *Centuries of Meditations* of Traherne a pointer to what we ourselves can do. We are not to do it his way but find our own. We have our own book to fill; we can follow his words, 'I have a mind to fill this with profitable wonders,' and we can start at once for this is the day we were given to do it in. We are in a world which is being remade every moment, we ourselves are such creatures of change, and true knowledge of this is the recognition of it that we are putting into prayer. Writing of the beauty of trees, Herbert Read spoke of the three hundred and sixty-five faces or facets in which in one year a tree presented its singular beauty to be observed. All genuine praying is part of a process of learning to be observant of such things. We may not be able in so short a lifetime to learn much, but all the more need to do what we can in a watchful condition, to be glad and grateful when somebody does open our eyes and ears, and to be ready to follow up the clues they give us.

The third feature may be related to the Benedictus, to the fact that God has visited His people. This has got to be noticed all over again in the particularities of history and the social scene in which we are now placed. The action of the Spirit doesn't make men and women puppets but responsible agents in the creative purpose of God. Preparation for prayer means scrutiny of this world scene in order that the response we make may be discerning as was that of Simeon and Anna when the moment of the presentation in the Temple came. The job of prayer is to turn the events into experience. It means that we have to be asking how what we encounter in the immediate circumstances in which we live and work, as well as in the world scene in which our life is to be lived out, can be turned into the material of dialogue with God. Our lives may be, as the world judges these things singularly uneventful, as plain and drab as it is possible to have, yet every moment is capable of being charged with perception of the Passion and the kind of engagement that at this moment is offered to us. But the Yes of such moments will never be made apart from the persistent plodding determination to use every scrap of its uneventfulness.

Uneventful or not, each human life undergoes great strain despite a great many devices to lighten or put off the burden. If praying is to be honest and unpretentious and not adding to the element of fantasy in life, it will be as much concerned with the shallows of living as with the depths. It is in the devouring shallows of trivial aimless insensitive living that most of us in any case get wrecked. Most of us can look back upon a great deal of wasted time and it is likely that increased leisure will intensify this problem, though 'laying waste our powers' is no new feature of human life. Looking forward alone does not of itself supply a remedy though it may offer its own variety of deceptive promise. It is the sense that so many clues have proved to be false, so many paths ended in getting nowhere, so many hopes exhausted, that breaks men and women who cannot be insensible to the shabbiness of their lives but find no enlivening alternative. Such people do not find the language of traditional devotion very helpful. It appears all too often to start from a point that they themselves are removed from, it presupposes a purity and an integrity that they are all too conscious of not possessing. To speak of the vision of God is often to add to the discouragement of those whose vision of life and of themselves is already clouded and murky. 'What should such fellows as I do crawling between heaven and earth?'

Does this make pious nonsense of a Yes to God? Does it split apart those who make much of prayer and those who stumble and stammer at it? Perhaps it needs saying first of all that God is not the possession of anyone, and those who have known this best have been most ready to warn us that not once but over and over again we may expect to find that the first are last and the last first, a picturesque way of saying that the best-intentioned can get it all wrong. We need to take very literally the point that we don't know how to pray as we ought, but not be put off by that. This is the real test. It cuts our attempted Yes to God down to the size that we don't much like but it doesn't pretend that No would do as well. A great deal of prayer in the depths found no better thing to do but to wait in silence, a silence that was not just a lack of words but a tacit assertion that God must speak first and that we must wait for that. How long must we wait? There again the record suggests that our time can give us no answer in hours or years but it can make known the presence of something we dare to call eternal in it. 'He will be present as He will be present,' that is, as and how He chooses to confront us with His Yes. 'In Him it is always Yes,' said St Paul, though he himself knew that such a word could throw a man dazed and blind to the ground and destroy all his self-assurance and set him to start all over again. Saying Yes to God then can be a squalid affair from which our stomachs rebel. That is a note of truth that the Psalmist knew very well. It gets an utterance nearer our time in Hopkins' poem 'Carrion Comfort' in which the poet cannot say Yes but will not say No. Carrion isn't sweet-smelling or elevating or a diet we take to, but we may have to live with it in this waiting for God. 'By this time he stinks,' said the sister of Lazarus very truthfully no doubt about the body of flesh of a dear brother, and we all of us shrink from some offensiveness that seems to negative all that we prized. To say that all our righteousness is as filthy rags is not difficult to do; to face the fact that our good-intentioned selves can stink is a painful and shocking thing. But Yes to God would lack its true weight and meaning if it could not start here from among the mire and clay and the smell of the pit, from the chaos that comes again and bespatters the form divine with filth, from the darkness that covers the world with fearful hatred and horror. Passion and engagement are knit together thus in the Yes God spoke to the world, and our attempted Yes of response cannot be otherwise spoken.

The end is not yet. Prayer is, however feeble and immature, a gesture of faith, the gesture we go on making in order that the

Yes of mankind may be uttered and known. Much of it must be like the irrelevant if well-meaning talking of Peter on the mount of transfiguration, much of it will be overtaken as were Peter's subsequent assertions of steadfastness by shabby and pitiful treachery, much of it will be and needs to be shaken out of its cherished illusions. But the faith that issues in prayer is, despite all these very real and grievous faults, a faith that perceives the glory of God and knows that the Yes He has spoken, the Yes that is Christ, is the truth to which it answers Amen.